Type 2 Diabetes Cookbook for Beginners

1800 Days of Healthy and Delicious Recipes Ready in 15 Minutes for People with Newly Diagnosed Type 2 Diabetes. 60-Day Meal Plan Included

Violet Harmond

Table of Contents

Introduction – Learning the Fundamentals of Diabetes

Many diseases and illnesses may lead to diabetes mellitus, a lifelong disorder. People with high blood sugar or glucose levels are affected. Although glucose is necessary to provide the body with energy, the hormone insulin, which is created by the pancreas, is required to transport glucose in circulation. If no insulin is present, glucose cannot be transported throughout the body and builds up in the blood. Therefore, a person is more likely to acquire diabetes at any stage if insulin is missing or present in insufficient amounts.

What is meant by Diabetes?

Diabetes as a chronic illness caused by either inadequate pancreatic insulin production or ineffective systemic insulin use. The hormone insulin regulates blood sugar levels.

Types of Diabetes

Understanding the forms and reasons for this chronic illness is crucial given that diabetes might be inescapable for most individuals, particularly if a person is obese or has a genetic history of the disease along with other risk factors for health.

There are three types of diabetes.

Type 1

Most cases of type 1 diabetes, commonly known as juvenile-onset diabetes, occur in children and teens.

Causes:

It happens when the body uses antibodies to fight its pancreas, causing the organ to be damaged and unable to generate insulin. The existence of damaged beta cells, which the pancreas requires to create insulin, might be another factor.

Because of these factors, Type 1 diabetes is recognized as entirely insulin-dependent and requires either needles or insulin pumps for administration.

Risk Factors:

- Pancreas damage caused by an infection, surgery, tumor, or accident.

- Physical strain from an operation or a sickness.

- Owning a sibling or parent or other family members with type 1 diabetes.

- Antibodies that erroneously target the organs or tissues within your own body are present.

- Exposure to virus-based diseases.

Type 2

Type 2 diabetes is the most prevalent type of diabetes. This kind, which affects over 95% of people, may have serious health effects if it is not adequately managed.

Causes:

Type 2 diabetes results from insufficient insulin production by the pancreas or insulin resistance in body cells. Those with insulin resistance and obesity are more likely to experience this. Although Type 2 is thought to be less difficult and aggressive than Type 1, diabetes in either form may be deadly if not treated with medication.

Risk Factors:

- Being a person of African, Hispanic, Asian, Native American, or Pacific Islander descent.

- Blood pressure is high.
- Becoming inactive physically.
- Gestational diabetes or having a baby that weighs more than nine pounds.
- A history of cardiovascular illness or a stroke.
- Family background sibling or parent with Type 2 diabetes or prediabetes.
- Being overweight or obese.
- Showing great triglyceride levels and low HDL cholesterol, or "excellent" cholesterol.
- 45 years of age or more.
- A polycystic ovary syndrome patient.
- Cigarette smoking.

Type 3

Pregnant women often get the final type of diabetes in their mid- to late periods.

Causes:

Genetic and environmental variables, as well as the hormone levels and physiological demands of pregnancy, are to blame. The infant might be harmed by the mother's elevated blood sugar levels, which circulate in the placenta. The great news is that a particular kind of diabetes is transient and will disappear after childbirth. However, studies reveal that around 10% of pregnant women having gestational diabetes subsequently acquire Type 2 diabetes.

Risk Factors:

- Being an American of African, Native, Hispanic, or Asian descent.
- Having reached the age of 25.
- Family history of Type 2 diabetes or prediabetes in a sibling or parent.
- Having been overweight or obese before becoming pregnant.

How to treat and manage diabetes?

There are several actions you may take to avoid diabetes.

It could be beneficial to perceive prediabetes as an incentive for making adjustments to help lower your risk rather than seeing it as a launching pad to diabetes.

The best way to prevent diabetes is to eat the correct foods and practice other lifestyle habits that support normal levels of insulin and blood sugar.

Is type 2 diabetes reversible?

Diabetes is a significant medical illness that is fairly frequent. Over 34 million Americans have diabetes, with 90 to 95% having type 2, as reported by the CDC (Centers for Disease Control and Prevention). Prediabetes precedes type 2 diabetes in over 88 million individuals.

Diabetes type 2 does not have a treatment. However, the disease could be reversible to the point where you no longer need medicine to control it, and your body is no longer adversely affected by possessing blood sugar levels that are excessively high.

The key to potentially curing or controlling type 2 diabetes is adopting healthy lifestyle changes, including eating a well-balanced diet, exercising frequently, and reaching and maintaining a healthy weight. Other lifestyle modifications, including giving up smoking, getting adequate sleep, reducing alcohol use, and stress management, may also be beneficial. But for other individuals, this is still insufficient, and they need medicine to treat their condition.

Can type 2 diabetes be cured?

Type 2 diabetes has no known treatment. However, research suggests that some individuals may be able to reverse it. You might be able to achieve and maintain normal blood glucose levels despite taking medication by making dietary adjustments and losing weight.

It does not imply that you have fully recovered. Diabetes type 2 is a chronic condition. There is always a possibility that signs will reappear, even if you are in remission, which means you are not taking any medication, but also the blood sugar levels remain within a healthy range. However, some individuals with diabetes can spend years without experiencing issues with glucose management or the associated health risks.

Losing weight may assist you in controlling diabetes, although, particularly if you've only suffered from the condition for a short time and haven't required insulin, it can lead to diabetes-free living.

Diabetes dietary needs

Contrary to common assumption, a diabetes type 2 diets should not always consist of a low-carbohydrate diet, nor must it include many high-protein foods or very few fats. The ADA advises focusing more on consuming a high-quality diet composed of whole, unprocessed foods and less on particular needs for proteins, carbohydrates, and fats.

The ideal calorie and portion amounts

A type 2 diabetic meal plan's food quantities are designed to fulfill your energy demands without ingesting too many extra calories stored as fat, resulting in unwelcome weight gain.

For those with diabetes, the precise amount of calories to eat each day depends on the quantity and scheduling of food that ensures you can maintain stable blood sugar levels and a healthy weight. Your age, level of exercise, frame size, present weight compared to your ideal weight, and other variables might affect that figure.

It might also be beneficial to consume most calories earlier in the day. According to recent studies, losing weight and improving blood sugar management is simpler if you have a substantial breakfast and a light lunch, ensuring that you have consumed most of your daily caloric intake by 3 p.m.

Food Combinations

Every meal or snack should have carbs, the most crucial strategy for regulating and maintaining blood sugar levels, along with some protein or fat. It implies that you won't feel hungry between foods and go for a fast fix, which would spike your blood sugar and lead your metabolism to store the extra calories as fat.

Fiber

Dietary fiber is the cornerstone of a healthy diet and the secret to any effective diabetic diet or weight-loss strategy.

Dietary fiber is the one element that distinguishes healthy carbohydrates from all other types of carbohydrates. Only plant-based foods are fiber-rich. Dried beans, lentils, peas, fruits, whole grains, vegetables, seeds, and nuts are among the foods with the greatest fiber.

For optimal health, a fiber-rich diet must include at least twenty-five to thirty-five grams of dietary fiber per day. For individuals with diabetes, fiber is crucial because it slows down the entry of all sugars into the circulation, including the ones formed naturally, such as those found in fruits and grains and any processed sugars you may eat.

Protein Options with Fewer Saturated Fats

Lean meats, seafood, poultry, low-fat dairy products, and eggs are excellent sources of high-quality protein for those who consume animal-derived foods. For part or all of their protein requirements, vegans, vegetarians, and non-vegetarians should resort to planting sources. Because they are low in carbohydrates, plant foods, including tempeh and soy-based tofu, are good sources of quasi-proteins and work well in a diabetic diet plan.

The same may be true for several whole-grain meals like kamut, quinoa, teff, nuts, and legumes, including black beans, lentils, chickpeas, and Edamame. Protein may be found in couscous and wild rice.

Carbs that Maintain Blood Sugar

It is more difficult to eat sensibly when you have diabetes because of the huge range of food items available today, each containing varying amounts and kinds of carbs. You should generally pick carbohydrates that have little to no effect on blood sugar. It entails choosing foods rich in fiber and low in glucose since they are absorbed gradually and hence have less influence on fluctuations in blood sugar levels. Consider beans, vegetables, fruits, whole-grain cereals and bread, dairy products, no added sugar, and beans.

Consuming less processed and prepared foods

In favor of whole, unprocessed foods, the ADA advises limiting the consumption of processed, prepared, refined, and quick meals. Typically, this entails cooking more of the own meals and dining in. It may not seem easy to shift to eating healthier home-cooked meals, but it requires little preparation.

Heart-friendly Fats

Diabetes increases your chance of acquiring other chronic health issues, including high blood pressure, kidney disease, and heart disease. Because of this, it's crucial to limit your consumption of saturated fat linked to heart problems and other illnesses and choose instead for heart-healthy unsaturated fats. Avocados, nuts, fatty fish, olive oil, seeds, and oils manufactured from nuts are all excellent sources of healthful fat.

Advice on transitioning to the diabetic diet

Simply keeping to regular mealtimes and consuming the best foods in moderation constitutes a diabetic diet.

A diabetic diet is a balanced, calorie- and fat-free eating regimen naturally high in nutrients. Fruits, vegetables, and whole grains are essential components. In actuality, a diabetic diet is the healthiest diet for the majority of people.

Why is it important to have a healthy eating strategy?

Your doctor will probably suggest you see a nutritionist to assist you in creating a healthy eating plan if you develop diabetes or prediabetes. The strategy aids in managing your weight, blood sugar, and risk for heart disease factors, including excessive blood pressure and fat levels.

Extra fat and calories cause your blood sugar to spike, which is not what you want. Lack of control of blood glucose may result in major issues, such as high blood glucose levels, that, if they continue, may cause long-term concerns, such as damage to the heart, kidneys, and nerves.

Making smart meal selections and keeping track of your eating patterns will help you maintain your blood glucose levels within a safe range.

Weight reduction has various additional health advantages and makes blood glucose management simpler for most persons with type 2 diabetes. A diabetic diet offers a well-planned, nourishing strategy to safely attain your goal if you have to reduce weight.

What is a diabetic diet composed of?

Eating three meals daily at regular intervals is the foundation of a diabetic diet. It improves how well you utilize the insulin your body makes or receives from a medicine.

You may create a diet depending on your health objectives, preferences, and lifestyle with the assistance of a trained dietitian. Additionally, they may advise you on changing your eating patterns, such as by picking portions appropriate for the size and level of exercise.

How to manage diabetes when it is first discovered

Eat healthily

Here is no each diet, and new diets might seem restrictive. It would help if you altered how much and what you consume, but much advice is available.

Keep in mind:

- Try to limit your food intake.
- Don't miss meals, and space them out evenly throughout the day.
- Consume a range of foods, such as lean meats or meat replacements, whole grains, fruits, vegetables, non-fat dairy products, and veggies.
- Avoid eating excessive amounts of one kind of food.

Get moving

Being active is another aspect of having diabetes and enjoying a healthy and full life. It doesn't matter what you're doing or how you go about it; physical exercise lowers blood sugar. Other advantages of exercise include:

- Reducing tension
- Reducing the chance of developing stroke and heart disease
- Possessing greater vigor
- Maintaining joint flexibility

If you have any concerns about appropriate activities, speak with your doctor. Among the beneficial physical activities to take into account are the following:

- Being active all day long and choosing the stairs over the elevator
- Stretching like exercises, yoga and stretching
- Aerobic exercise like swimming, biking, and walking
- Lifting weights or utilizing resistance bands for strength training

Ingest your medication

A further tool for treating type 2 diabetes is medication. Consult your doctor to determine which medications may help you maintain blood sugar levels within the desired range. Some individuals take insulin by themselves, while others combine it with tablets.

Ask your pharmacist, doctor, or diabetes educator pertinent questions before starting new medications.

FAQ

1. What are type 2 diabetes first warning signs?

The most typical early symptoms of type 2 diabetes might include weight gain and exhaustion, but unexpectedly they can also include low blood sugar sensations.

2. What type 2 diabetes signs and symptoms are there?

Type 2 diabetes symptoms are as diverse as they are uncomfortable.

3. What signs and symptoms might a man have of type 2 diabetes?

Along with the symptoms regularly mentioned, erectile dysfunction is a different problem that is less typically brought up.

4. Which foods contribute to type 2 diabetes?

Research supports the idea that specific diets, such as grain products and sugary drinks, may raise the risk of type 2 diabetes.

5. Why does type 2 diabetes occur?

Both genes and the environment may bring on type 2 diabetes.

6. What symptoms might indicate diabetes?

There are many methods for diagnosing type 2 diabetes. These include increased glucose levels on an oral tolerance test, a fast glucose of greater or Equal to 126 mg/dL, and a hemoglobin A1C of at least 6.5%.

7. What signs and symptoms do women with type 2 diabetes exhibit?

A polycystic ovarian syndrome is a prevalent condition reported in women having type 2 diabetes or prediabetes (PCOS).

8. What distinguishes type 1 from type 2 diabetes?

The inability of the body to manufacture insulin is the outcome of type 1 diabetes, an autoimmune illness.

9. How can type 2 diabetes be prevented?

Contacting a primary care physician is one of the most crucial initial measures to avoid type 2 diabetes.

10. How are type 2 diabetes and prediabetes managed with metformin?

It's interesting to note that the precise mechanism of activity of metformin remains unknown. Despite indicating that other mechanisms could be involved, it seems to decrease the liver's ability to produce glucose.

Shopping list

A wholesome, well-balanced diet may help you manage type 2 diabetes or prediabetes. Foods from all dietary categories, such as fruits, whole grains, vegetables, legumes, and dairy, should be included in meals and snacks.

Foods to Eat

Vegetable and Fruits

Tip: Choose vegetables and fruits in a range of colors. Non-starchy vegetables are the lowest in calories and carbohydrates. Count the carbs in your starchy vegetables and fruits just as you would for any carbohydrate food group.

Non-starchy Vegetables:

- Cauliflower
- Green Beans
- Asparagus
- Salad Greens
- Zucchini
- Broccoli
- Brussels sprouts
- Eggplant
- Celery
- Carrots

Fresh Fruits:

- Bananas
- Oranges
- Watermelon
- Avocado
- Berries
- Apples
- Grapefruit
- Cantaloupe

Starchy Vegetables:

- Corn
- Winter Squash
- Sweet Potatoes

Canned foods:

Tip: Choose fruits packed in juice, not syrup, and look for low sodium vegetables.

- Vegetables
- Fruits
- Beans

Frozen foods:

Tip: Read the nutrient label to avoid products with lot of sugar, additives, or sodium.

- Vegetables
- Shrimp or Fish
- Fruits

- Desserts (single-serving)

Breakfast snacks and cereals:

Tip: Look for the words "whole-wheat", "sprouted grain", "whole-grain", and "high-fiber". Choose foods with at least 3 grams of dietary fiber and fewer than 8 grams of sugar per serving.

- Crackers
- Nuts
- Cereal
- Snack Bars

Legumes:

Tip: Because they're similar enough in nutrients, you can include any legumes you like in your diet.

- Peanuts
- Lentils
- Beans
- Peas

Seafood and Meat:

Tips: Try to plan at least two servings of fish each week. Also aim to fit three servings of lean meat into your meal plan every week.

- Chicken
- Lean meat
- Fatty fish
- Turkey Breast

Grains:

Tip: Look for the words "oats", "corn", "quinoa", and "buckwheat".

- Pasta
- Rice
- Bread
- Oatmeal

Dairy and dairy alternatives:

Tip: Try non-dairy products, such as those made with flax, soy, hemp, or almond. Watch out for added sugars in yogurts.

- Milk
- Greek yogurt or yogurt
- Cottage cheese

Foods to Avoid

Simple carbs, saturated fats, and Trans fats should not be consumed in considerable quantities by anybody eating a low or extremely low-carbohydrate diet.

Cakes, candies, and ice cream all contain sugar.

People should minimize their consumption of the following items:

- Packaged and quick meals, including baked goods, candies, chips, and desserts.
- White rice and pasta
- Sweet cereals
- Refined meats
- Sliced bread
- French fries and other fried meals
- Sugary beverages
- A red meat

Avoiding low-fat foods that include sugar instead of fat is also a good idea. Yogurt without fat is a nice illustration.

People with type 2 diabetes or prediabetes may want to consider replacing some of their favorite meals with healthier alternatives. It can include picking whole-grain pasta, bread, or rice or switching out fried potatoes for baked ones.

The best alternative is to prepare meals at home since it enables one to avoid the added sugars in many prepared foods.

This book includes 200 recipes to help you maintain a diabetic diet.

Chapter 1: Breakfast Recipes

Spinach, Greek Cheese, and Olive Omelet

(Preparation Time: 3 minutes | Cooking Time: 8 minutes | Serving 2 | Difficulty: Easy)

Ingredients:

- 2 beaten eggs
- 14g or 2 tablespoons kasseri cheese, shredded
- 4 Kalamata olives, chopped and pitted
- 15 ml or 1 tablespoon olive oil
- 20g or 2 tablespoons feta cheese, crumbled
- 28 g or ½ cup spinach or baby spinach leaves, freshly chopped

Instructions:

1. Use olive oil as the fat while preparing your omelet.
2. The cheeses should be layered on the spinach, followed by the chopped olives.
3. Allow it to simmer until the cheese is heated and the spinach is just beginning to wilt.

Nutritional Info: 529 cal, 37g fat (17g sag. fat), 620mg chol, 1033mg sod, 17g carb (4.3g sugars, 7.8g fiber), 37g pro.

Oatmeal Superfoods Breakfast

(Preparation Time: 5 minutes | Cooking Time: 10 minutes | Serving 2 | Difficulty: Easy)

Ingredients:

- ½ cup oatmeal, dry
- 2 tsp. sunflower seeds
- 1 tsp. cocoa
- 2 tsp. Flax seeds, ground
- A dash cinnamon

Instructions:

1. Oatmeal is cooked in boiling water; the other ingredients are combined.
2. If necessary, add a couple of drops of the lucuma powder to sweeten.
3. Chia seeds or pumpkin seeds may be used instead of sunflower seeds.
4. Instead of chocolate, you might add a few blueberries or other fruit.

Nutritional Info: 270 cal, 9g fat (1g sag. fat), 5mg chol, 95mg sod, 41g carb (10g sugars, 6g fiber), 9g pro.

Tortilla

(Preparation Time: 5 minutes | Cooking Time: 25 minutes | Serving 2 | Difficulty: Easy)

Ingredients:

- 1 turnip, medium
- 30 to 45 ml or 2-3 tablespoons olive oil divided
- Ground black pepper and salt, for taste
- ¼ head of cauliflower
- 1 thinly sliced onion, medium
- 6 eggs
- Optional: Fresh parsley, chopped

Instructions:

1. Set your broiler to low heat.

2. Slice your cauliflower thinly, including the stem, and slice your turnip thinly after peeling it. They should be placed in a microwave-safe casserole with a little covered water and microwaved on high for 6 to 7 minutes.

3. Meanwhile, begin sautéing the onion in two tablespoons of olive oil in a nonstick pan that is 8 to 9 inches in size. Give your skillet a spritz of nonstick cooking spray if it isn't already nonstick. Use moderate heat.

4. Take the vegetables out of the microwave when it beeps, drain them, and then put them in the pan with the onion. For 10 to 15 minutes, or until the vegetables turn golden around the edges, continue sautéing it all, adding a little more oil if anything starts to stick. Spread the veggies evenly over the bottom of the pan and lower the heat.

5. Pour the eggs over the veggies after combining them with salt and pepper.

6. Lift the edges commonly to allow the uncooked egg to run underneath while cooking on reduced for five to seven minutes. Slide its skillet below a low broiler for four to five minutes to ensure that the top of the tortilla is golden once everything is cooked except for the top.

7. To serve, cut into wedges. It's great to add some parsley, but it's not necessary.

Nutritional Info: 237 cal, 1g fat (0.3g sag. fat), 5mg chol, 482mg sod, 50g carb (2.8g sugars, 2.4g fiber), 7g pro.

Avocado and Monterey Jack Omelet

(Preparation Time: 5 minutes | Cooking Time: 2 minutes | Serving 2 | Difficulty: Easy)

Ingredients:

- 2 teaspoons butter
- ½ sliced avocado
- 2 beaten eggs
- 28 g (1 ounce) Monterey Jack cheese, shredded or sliced

Instructions:

1. Prepare your omelet.

2. Turn the heat low, add your cheese, cover the pan, and let the cheese melt.

3. Right before folding, add sliced avocado.

Nutritional Info: 372 cal, 32g fat (2.9g sag. fat), 5.3mg chol, 468.5mg sod, 16.5g carb (3.2g sugars, 8.1g fiber), 24.6g pro.

Frittata

(Preparation Time: 5 minutes | Cooking Time: 10 minutes | Serving 2 | Difficulty: Easy)

Ingredients:

- ½ sliced zucchini
- 1 tbsp. Green onions, sliced
- Pepper and salt to taste
- 2 eggs
- 1 tbsp. avocado or olive oil
- ¼ cup torn spinach, fresh
- ¼ tsp. garlic, crushed
- 1/8 cup coconut milk

Instructions:

1. In a pan over medium heat, warm the olive oil. Cook the zucchini until it is soft.

2. Garlic, spinach, and green onions are combined. Add salt and pepper to taste. Cook the spinach a little longer until it wilts.

3. Coconut milk and eggs should be combined in a different dish. Pour over the veggies in the skillet.

4. Cook eggs until hard over low heat with a lid.

Nutritional Info: 291 cal, 20g fat (9.4g sag. fat), 320mg chol, 1028mg sod, 4.4g carb (1.6g sugars, 0.5g fiber), 24g pro.

Club Omelet

(Preparation Time: 5 minutes | Cooking Time: 5 minutes | Serving 2 | Difficulty: Easy)

Ingredients:

- 55g or 2 ounces turkey breast, sliced
- 1 scallion
- 14 g or 1 tablespoon mayonnaise

- 2 bacon slices
- ½ tomato, small
- 2 eggs

Instructions:

1. You may either cook & drain the bacon or crumble it in the microwave.

2. Slice the scallion and tomato, and then cut the turkey into tiny squares.

3. Making an omelet using beaten eggs and a few spoonful's of bacon fat.

4. The turkey and bacon should only be added at this point.

5. When it's done to your preference, top the meat with the scallion and tomato, spread your mayonnaise on the opposite side, fold it over, and serve.

Nutritional Info: 579 cal, 22g fat (12g sag. fat), 280mg chol, 774mg sod, 65g carb (3g sugars, 3g fiber), 30g pro.

Yogurt Oatmeal Breakfast

(Preparation Time: 20 minutes | Cooking Time: 0 minutes | Serving 2 | Difficulty: Easy)

Ingredients:

- Optional: Handful of blueberries
- ½ cup oatmeal, dry
- 1 cup yogurt, low-fat

Instructions:

1. When using steel-cut oats, combine all ingredients and let sit for 20 minutes or overnight in the refrigerator.

Nutritional Info: 260 cal, 3.5g fat (0.5g sag. fat), 5mg chol, 112.5mg sod, 46.2g carb (9g sugars, 4g fiber), 11.3g pro.

Asparagus All'uovo

(Preparation Time: 5 minutes | Cooking Time: 15 minutes | Serving 2 | Difficulty: Easy)

Ingredients:

- 1 crushed clove garlic
- Ground black pepper and salt, to taste
- 8 eggs

- 455 g or 1 pound asparagus
- 60 ml or ¼ cup olive oil
- 50 g or ½ cup Parmesan cheese, grated

Instructions:

1. Set the broiler on high.

2. Asparagus bottoms should be cut off where they naturally break. Put the asparagus stalks in a crystal pie plate or a casserole dish that can be microwaved. Cover after adding a few teaspoons of water. Three to four minutes on high in the microwave.

3. Crush the garlic and add it to the olive oil while the asparagus cooks.

4. Drain the asparagus after it is finished. This recipe works well with four long, oval, single-serving ovenproof gratin plates. Among the 2 plates, distribute the asparagus. If not, a rectangle glass baking dish must be used. Place the asparagus inside the baking dish in 4 groupings.

5. Every serving of asparagus should be drizzled with garlic oil, using individual plates or one baking dish. The cheese should be divided into 2 portions with a mild salt and pepper sprinkling. Lay the asparagus 4 inches above low heat under the broiler. For four to five minutes, broil it.

6. Fry the eggs to your preference, whereas the asparagus are broiling. Either cook them everything at once in your largest pan or split them between two skillets.

7. Remove the asparagus from the broiler once the Parmesan begins to turn golden. Use a large spatula to delicately move each serving of fresh asparagus to the plate if you baked it all at once. Add two fried eggs to the top of each asparagus dish before serving.

Nutritional Info: 112 cal, 1g fat (0.6g sag. fat), 0mg chol, 3mg sod, 5.2g carb (2.5g sugars, 1g fiber), 2.9g pro.

Buffalo Wing Sauce Omelet

(Preparation Time: 5 minutes | Cooking Time: 8 minutes | Serving 2 | Difficulty: Easy)

Ingredients:

- 2 beaten eggs
- 14g or 1 tablespoon butter
- 1 ½ teaspoons of bacon grease
- 24g or 3 tablespoons blue cheese, crumbled
- 15 ml or 1 tablespoon hot sauce

Instructions:

1. Use the bacon grease as that of the fat while preparing your omelet. Put the blue cheese inside.

2. Heat the butter and hot sauce inside a small pot or microwave for one minute inside custard cup while your omelet is being covered at low heat and melting the cheese.

3. Fold and dish the finished omelet, add the sauce on top, and serve.

4. Yummy!

Nutritional Info: 378 cal, 26.6g fat (8.3g sag. fat), 420mg chol, 795mg sod, 3g carb (2g sugars, 0g fiber), 27g pro.

Monterey Scramble

(Preparation Time: 3 minutes | Cooking Time: 5 minutes | Serving 2 | Difficulty: Easy)

Ingredients:

- 2 scallions
- 3 eggs
- 14 g or 1 tablespoon butter
- 2 artichoke hearts, canned
- 28 g 1 ounce Monterey Jack cheese
- 1 teaspoon pesto sauce

Instructions:

1. Artichoke hearts, cheese, and scallions should all be thinly sliced and ready to go.

2. Your eggs should be scrambled while the pesto is mixed in entirely.

3. Spray some nonstick cooking spray in your medium skillet and heat it to medium-high. Melt the butter after adding it.

4. Place the vegetables in the pan and then pour the eggs over them.

5. Combine everything and stir when the eggs are nearly cooked to your preference. Spread the cheese on top, cover the pan, extinguish the flame, and allow the residual heat to melt your cheese and complete the egg-cooking process.

Nutritional Info: 430 cal, 20g fat (9g sag. fat), 60mg chol, 1.4mg sod, 46g carb (3g sugars, 2g fiber), 14g pro.

Rodeo Eggs

(Preparation Time: 5 minutes | Cooking Time: 10 minutes | Serving 2 | Difficulty: Easy)

Ingredients:

- 4 slices of onion, thinly sliced
- 4 Cheddar cheese, thinly sliced
- 4 bacon, 1 inch chopped slices
- 4 eggs

Instructions:

1. Start frying the bacon in a large, heavy skillet at medium heat. Push it away and add the onion pieces once some fat has cooked off. Fry the onion until it becomes transparent on each side, gently flipping it to retain the slices together. The onion should be taken out of the pan and put aside.

2. The bacon should be cooked in batches until crisp. Most of the fat should have drained out, then scattered the bacon pieces around the skillet's bottom. The eggs should be cracked in and cooked for a few minutes; when the bottoms are cooked, the tops are always runny.

3. Over each yolk, place a piece of onion. Next, top the onion and a slice of cheese. When the cheese is completely melted, add a teaspoon more water to the pan, cover it, and simmer for 2 to 3 minutes. Serve after cutting with the edge of the spatula into 4 distinct pieces.

Nutritional Info: 77 cal, 5.3g fat (1.6g sag. fat), 212mg chol, 210mg sod, 0.6g carb (0.2g sugars, 0g fiber), 6.3g pro.

California Omelet

(Preparation Time: 5 minutes | Cooking Time: 6 minutes | Serving 2 | Difficulty: Easy)

Ingredients:

- 2 beaten eggs
- ¼ sliced avocado
- 15 ml or 1 tablespoon olive oil
- 55 g or 2 ounces shredded Monterey Jack cheese
- 4g or ¼ cup alfalfa sprouts

Instructions:

1. Once you're ready to add your filling, prepare your omelet and spread the Monterey Jack across half of it.

2. Cook with the lid for 2 to 3 minutes, and then reduce the heat to low.

3. After placing the avocado with sprouts on top of the cheese, continue preparing the omelet as directed.

Nutritional Info: 308.5 cal, 17g fat (5.4g sag. fat), 217.5mg chol, 534.6mg sod, 9.7g carb (4.3g sugars, 3.3g fiber), 30g pro.

Backward Pizza

(Preparation Time: 5 minutes + Cooking in the oven (12 minutes) | Serving 2 | Difficulty: Easy)

Ingredients:

- 45 ml or 3 tablespoons olive oil
- 1 ½ teaspoon oregano, dried
- 25 g or ¼ cup Parmesan cheese, grated
- 1 clove garlic
- 80 g or 1/3 cup pizza sauce, without sugar
- Optional: ½ teaspoon red pepper flakes

Instructions:

1. Turn on the 375°F oven. Use nonstick foil to line a gelatin roll pan.

2. To the corners of the foil, equally, distribute the mozzarella. You would want the cheese to be golden brown throughout. Bake for about 5 minutes; flip the pan to let it cook evenly, then bake for 5 to 7 minutes.

3. Crush your garlic into a small cup, add the olive oil, and whisk once as the cheese bakes.

4. Pizza sauce should be warmed up in the microwave for one minute.

5. Take the cheese from the oven when it has a uniform, golden coating. Use a brush or the back of the spoon to distribute the garlicky oil across the surface. If using, top with red pepper flakes and oregano.

6. Over oil, spread your pizza sauce, and then top with the Parmesan. To serve, cut the cake into 6 large rectangles.

Nutritional Info: 252 cal, 13g fat (5.8g sag. fat), 29mg chol, 482mg sod, 22g carb (2.6g sugars, 1.7g fiber), 11.8g pro.

Goat Cheese and Smoked Salmon Scramble

(Preparation Time: 5 minutes | Cooking Time: 10 minutes | Serving 2 | Difficulty: Easy)

Ingredients:

- 120 ml or ½ cup heavy cream
- 4 scallions
- 115 g or 4 ounces of moist salmon, smoked
- 4 eggs
- 1 teaspoon dill weed, dried
- 115 g or 4 ounces goat cheese (chèvre)
- 14 to 28 g or 1 to 2 tablespoons butter

Instructions:

1. Together with the dill and cream, whisk your eggs.

2. Scallions should be thinly sliced, even the crisp green portion. Cut the chèvre into small chunks; it will resemble cream cheese in texture. Crumble your smoked salmon coarsely.

3. Melt your butter into a large, preferably nonstick pan over medium-high heat.

4. Add your scallions and cook them for a minute after the butter has melted.

5. Add the egg mixture, and heat it for 60 to 90 seconds, constantly stirring, to ensure that the eggs are partially set.

6. Once the eggs are set, add the chèvre with smoked salmon and finish cooking and stirring the mixture.

Nutritional Info: 331 cal, 24g fat (12g sag. fat), 411mg chol, 557mg sod, 1g carb (1g sugars, 0g fiber), 25g pro.

Cocoa Oatmeal

(Preparation Time: 5 minutes | Cooking Time: 10 minutes | Serving 2 | Difficulty: Easy)

Ingredients:

- 1 cup water
- ½ tsp. vanilla bean, ground
- 1 tbsp. lucuma powder
- 1 dash cinnamon
- ½ cup oats, dry
- 1 pinch tsp. salt
- 1 tbsp. cocoa powder
- 3 tbsp. flax seeds meal, ground
- 2 egg whites

Instructions:

1. The salt and oats should be combined in a pot over high heat. Submerge in water. Stirring periodically, boil and then simmer for three to five minutes.

2. As the mixture thickens, continue additional ½ cup water if required.

3. To make a smooth sauce, combine 1 tablespoon. Cocoa powder with 4 tablespoons. Water in another dish. In the pan, whisk in the vanilla.

4. Lower the temperature. Add the egg whites, and then start whisking right away. Cinnamon and flax meal should be added. To blend, stir.

5. Remove from the fire, stir in the lucuma powder, and serve immediately.

6. Sliced blueberries, strawberries, or a few almonds are suggested toppings.

Nutritional Info: 160 cal, 3g fat (1g sag. fat), 0mg chol, 0mg sod, 30g carb (16g sugars, 11g fiber), 6g pro.

Braunschweiger Omelet

(Preparation Time: 5 minutes | Cooking Time: 5 minutes | Serving 2 | Difficulty: Easy)

Ingredients:

- 2 beaten eggs
- ¼ ripe tomato, medium sliced
- 14 g or 1 tablespoon butter
- 55 g 2 ounces Braunschweiger, mashed using a fork
- Optional: Mayonnaise

Instructions:

1. When assembling your omelet, spread the mashed Braunschweiger across half and add the tomato slices over the top.

2. A spoonful of mayonnaise is an excellent addition if you want to embellish it.

Nutritional Info: 93 cal, 8.1g fat (2.6g sag. fat), 51mg chol, 277mg sod, 0.9g carb (0g sugars, 0g fiber), 4.1g pro.

Blueberry and Flax Vanilla Overnight Oats

(Preparation Time: 5 minutes | Cooking Time: 0 minutes | Serving 2 | Difficulty: Easy)

Ingredients:

- 1/3 cup water
- ½ tsp. vanilla bean, ground
- 1 pinch salt
- ½ cup oats, dry
- ½ cup yogurt, low-fat
- 2 tbsp. Flax seeds meal
- Blueberries, blackberries, almonds, and lucuma powder for topping

Instructions:

1. In the evening, add all the ingredients to the bowl but the toppings.

2. Overnight refrigerate.

3. Stir the ingredients in the morning. It must be substantial. Choose your favorite toppings to add.

Nutritional Info: 345 cal, 4g fat (2g sag. fat), 6mg chol, 671mg sod, 56g carb (20g sugars, 7g fiber), 13g pro.

Rosemary-Parmesan Eggs

(Preparation Time: 3 minutes | Cooking Time: 5 minutes | Serving 2 | Difficulty: Easy)

Ingredients:

- 50 g or ½ cup Parmesan cheese, grated
- 1 teaspoon rosemary, ground
- 14 g or 1 tablespoon butter
- 6 eggs
- 60 ml or ¼ cup heavy cream
- 1 crushed clove garlic

Instructions:

1. The cheese, eggs, cream, garlic, and rosemary are all whisked together. Heat a sizable skillet to a moderate setting.

2. Pour that egg mixture into the heated pan after adding the butter and stirring it one more to ensure that the cheese hasn't sunk to the bottom.

3. Serve the eggs scrambled after they have set.

Nutritional Info: 530 cal, 23g fat (9g sag. fat), 375mg chol, 1630mg sod, 43g carb (5g sugars, 2g fiber), 33g pro.

Apple Oatmeal

(Preparation Time: 5 minutes | Cooking Time: 5 minutes | Serving 2 | Difficulty: Easy)

Ingredients:

- ½ cup oats, dry
- 1 dash cinnamon
- ½ apple, grated
- 1 cups water
- 1 tsp. lucuma powder

Instructions:

1. For three to five minutes, cook the oats in the water.

2. Add cinnamon and apple gratings. Add the lucuma powder and stir.

Nutritional Info: 240 cal, 3g fat (1g sag. fat), 45mg chol, 170mg sod, 35g carb (10g sugars, 4g fiber), 20g pro.

Instant Quiche

(Preparation Time: 5 minutes | Cooking Time: 15 minutes | Serving 2 | Difficulty: Easy)

Ingredients:

- 5 eggs
- 60 ml or ¼ cup milk, carb-reduced
- ½ teaspoon salt
- 1 pinch of nutmeg, ground
- 225 g or 8 ounces of Swiss cheese, shredded
- 8 bacon slices
- 60 ml or ¼ cup heavy cream
- 15 ml or 1 tablespoon vermouth, dry
- ¼ teaspoon black pepper, ground
- 14 g or 1 tablespoon butter

Instructions:

1. Over medium heat, place a ten-inch nonstick skillet. Heat it.

2. Place the bacon in a microwave-safe baking dish or on a bacon rack.

3. Please put it in the microwave for eight to nine minutes on high.

4. Whisk the cream, eggs, carb-reduced milk, salt, vermouth, pepper, and then nutmeg in a wide mixing bowl.

5. Once the butter melts and coats the bottom of your now-hot pan, swirl it around. Now add the egg mixture. Pull aside the section of the set egg and allow the liquid egg to flow below while you gently stir your eggs with a spatula. Ideally, one made for nonstick skillets. It won't function like an omelet, where the edges harden solid enough to raise the entire thing. Gently stir them until they are approximately halfway between liquid and set.

6. Evenly distribute the eggs in the pan, and then top with the shredded cheese. Turn the flame to low and cover the skillet. Set the rack four inches underneath the broiler after turning it on.

7. Once the bacon is finished cooking, remove it, drain it, and give it a minute or two to cool. After that, crumble it or, for a simpler option, cut it into pieces with kitchen shears. Then, evenly distribute the bacon pieces on top of the Instant Quiche.

8. Once the top is set, place everything in the broiler for a minute. After that, slice it into wedges to serve.

Nutritional Info: 298 cal, 20g fat (8.8g sag. fat), 99mg chol, 332mg sod, 17g carb (2.9g sugars, 1.6g fiber), 12.5g pro.

Egg pizza crust

(Preparation Time: 5 minutes | Cooking Time: 5 minutes | Serving 2 | Difficulty: Easy)

Ingredients:

- ¼ cup coconut flour
- 1 small garlic clove, crushed
- 2 eggs
- ½ cup coconut milk

Instructions:

1. Make an omelet by combining.

Nutritional Info: 197 cal, 9g fat (4.5g sag. fat), 21.5mg chol, 648mg sod, 5.8g carb (1.8g sugars, 0.5g fiber), 22.1g pro.

Pomegranate Coconut Oatmeal

(Preparation Time: 5 minutes | Cooking Time: 5 minutes | Serving 2 | Difficulty: Easy)

Ingredients:

- 1/3 cup coconut milk
- 2 tbs. shredded coconut, unsweetened
- 1 tbs. lucuma powder
- ½ cup oats, dry
- 1 cups water
- 1 tbs. flax seeds meal
- 4 tbs. pomegranate seeds

Instructions:

1. Salt, water, and coconut milk are used for cooking the oats.

2. Add the flaxseed meal, coconut, and lucuma powder by stirring. Add more pomegranate seeds and coconut as garnish.

Nutritional Info: 234 cal, 3g fat (1g sag. fat), 5mg chol, 8mg sod, 29g carb (38g sugars, 11g fiber), 8g pro.

Omelet with veggies

(Preparation Time: 5 minutes | Cooking Time: 5 minutes | Serving 2 | Difficulty: Easy)

Ingredients:

- Salt
- 1 tsp. cumin or olive oil
- 1 spoon of yogurt cheese
- 1 pinch dill (optional)
- 2 eggs, large
- Ground black pepper
- 1 cups cherry tomatoes and spinach
- Red pepper flakes, crushed

Instructions:

1. In a bowl, whisk 2 big eggs. Set aside after seasoning with salt and freshly ground black pepper in a medium pan set over medium heat, warm 1 teaspoon of olive oil. Add cheese, tomatoes, and baby spinach when the spinach has wilted.

2. Add the eggs; simmer, stirring periodically, for approximately a minute or until set. Add cheese and stir. Add dill and red pepper flakes that have been crushed.

Nutritional Info: 180 cal, 2g fat (1g sag. fat), 3mg chol, 357mg sod, 1.7g carb (1.3g sugars, 0.3g fiber), 9.8g pro.

Egg Muffins

(Preparation Time: 5 minutes | Cooking Time: 5 minutes | Serving 2 | Difficulty: Easy)

Ingredients:

- ½ cup green bell pepper, diced
- ¼ tsp. salt
- 2 tbsp. water
- 4 eggs
- ½ cup onion, diced
- ½ cup spinach
- 1/8 tsp. Black pepper, ground

Instructions:

1. Preheat oven to 350 degrees Fahrenheit. Oil four muffin tins. Combined egg beating Bell pepper, onion, spinach, salt, water, and black pepper should all be combined.

2. Fill the muffin tins with the mixture. Bake muffins in the oven once they are done throughout.

Nutritional Info: 137 cal, 10g fat (3g sag. fat), 193mg chol, 328mg sod, 3g carb (1g sugars, 2g fiber), 9g pro.

Steak and Eggs

(Preparation Time: 5 minutes | Cooking Time: 10 minutes | Serving 2 | Difficulty: Easy)

Ingredients:

- ¼ tsp. black pepper, ground
- 1 tsp. coconut oil
- ½ diced red bell pepper
- 1 egg
- ¼ lb. pork tenderloin or beef steak, boneless

- ¼ tsp. sea salt (optional)
- ¼ diced onion
- 1 handful of augural or spinach

Instructions:

1. Black pepper and sea salt are used to season pork tenderloin or sliced steak. A sauté pan is hot to the touch. When the pan is heated, add 1 teaspoon coconut oil, the onions, and the meat. Sauté until the steak is just cooked.

2. Add spinach with red bell pepper when the steak is cooked to your preference. In the meanwhile, preheat a little frying pan over medium heat. Fry two eggs in the remaining coconut oil. Serve steak topped with a fried egg.

Nutritional Info: 390 cal, 25g fat (7g sag. fat), 472mg chol, 221mg sod, 3g carb (1g sugars, 0g fiber), 33g pro.

Salmon Smoked Scrambled Eggs

(Preparation Time: 5 minutes | Cooking Time: 8 minutes | Serving 2 | Difficulty: Easy)

Ingredients:

- 2 eggs
- 2 oz. sliced smoked salmon
- 1 tsp. black pepper, ground to taste
- 1 tsp. coconut oil
- 1 tbsp. water
- ¼ avocado
- 2 minced chives

Instructions:

1. A skillet should be heated to medium. When coconut oil is heated, add it to the pan. In the meanwhile, scramble eggs. Add smoked salmon and eggs to the heated skillet. Cook eggs till frothy and soft while stirring often. Get rid of the heat.

2. To serve, sprinkle chives, black pepper, and avocado on top.

Nutritional Info: 205 cal, 12g fat (4g sag. fat), 380mg chol, 404mg sod, 2g carb (1g sugars, 0g fiber), 18g pro.

Egg Bake

(Preparation Time: 5 minutes | Cooking Time: 40 minutes | Serving 2 | Difficulty: Easy)

Ingredients:

- ¼ cup zucchini
- ¼ cup green onions, sliced
- ¼ cup coconut milk
- 1 tbsp. fresh parsley, minced
- 1/8 tsp. Salt
- ½ cup spinach or red peppers, chopped
- ½ tbsp. coconut oil
- 2 eggs
- 1/8 cup almond flour
- ¼ tsp. basil, dried
- 1/8 tsp. Black pepper, ground

Instructions:

1. Set oven to 350 degrees Fahrenheit. In a skillet, add coconut oil. Set the heat to medium. When the veggies are ready, add the mushrooms, onions, zucchini, and red pepper and cook for approximately 5 minutes. Vegetables should be drained and placed over the baking dish.

2. Whisk together the eggs, flour, milk, parsley, salt, basil, and pepper in a bowl. Place baking dish with egg mixture inside.

3. Bake in a preheated oven for about thirty-five to forty minutes or until the middle is set.

Nutritional Info: 140 cal, 10g fat (3g sag. fat), 370mg chol, 120mg sod, 1g carb (1g sugars, 0g fiber), 12g pro.

Zucchini Pancakes

(Preparation Time: 5 minutes | Baking Time: 10 minutes | Serving 2 | Difficulty: Easy)

Ingredients:

- 1 tbsp. onion, chopped
- 3 tbsp. almond flour
- ½ tsp. black pepper, ground
- 1 zucchini, small
- 2 eggs, beaten
- ½ tsp. salt
- Coconut oil

Instructions:

1. Preheat oven to 300 degrees Fahrenheit.

2. Add the eggs and onion to the grated zucchini in a bowl. Add salt, pepper, and 6 tbsp. of flour.

3. Coconut oil is added to a wide sauté pan that has been heated to medium-high heat. Reduce the heat to moderate after the oil is heated, then pour the batter into the pan. The pancakes should be cooked for approximately Two minutes on each side. Pancakes should be baked.

Nutritional Info: 69 cal, 3g fat (1g sag. fat), 3mg chol, 153mg sod, 7g carb (1g sugars, 1g fiber), 4g pro.

Pancakes Naan Crepes

(Preparation Time: 5 minutes | Cooking Time: 10 minutes | Serving 2 | Difficulty: Easy)

Ingredients:

- ½ cup Tapioca Flour
- Salt
- ½ cup almond flour
- 1 cup coconut milk
- Coconut oil

Instructions:

1. All the components should be combined.

2. Pour batter into a hot pan until it reaches the required thickness. Flip the batter over to heat the second side once it seems firm.

3. Leave off the salt if you want a sweet crepe or pancake. If you'd like, you may include some spices, minced ginger or garlic, or both in the batter.

Nutritional Info: 120 cal, 6g fat (0g sag. fat), 0mg chol, 10mg sod, 13g carb (1g sugars, 1g fiber), 2g pro.

Chapter 2: Grains and Beans Recipes

Green Braised Beans and Pork

(Preparation Time: 5 minutes | Cooking Time: 12 minutes | Serving 2 | Difficulty: Easy)

Ingredients:

- 1 finely chopped onion
- ½ inch fresh ginger, peeled and sliced
- 2 roughly chopped tomatoes
- 1 cup chicken broth
- ¼ lemons, wedges cut for serving
- 2 cups green beans, frozen or fresh
- 2 garlic cloves, thinly sliced
- ½ tsp. red pepper flakes, more for taste
- 2 tbsp. coconut oil
- Ground black pepper and salt
- 10 oz. lean pork

Instructions:

1. Melt the coconut oil inside a skillet by halving each bean over medium heat. Over medium heat, sauté the garlic, onion, and ginger until they are tender.
2. Sauté the tomatoes and red pepper after adding them until the tomato starts to wilt. Add the green beans and stir. Add lean pork cubes. Over medium heat, add the broth and bring it to a boil.
3. To become tender, the beans must simmer for 10 minutes in a pressure cooker. Use pepper and salt as needed to season. Lemon wedges should be served on the side.

Nutritional Info: 143 cal, 4.3g fat (1.1g sag. fat), 42.5mg chol, 73.2mg sod, 9.9g carb (2.2g sugars, 2.3g fiber), 16.8g pro.

Lentil Easy Dal

(Preparation Time: 5 minutes | Cooking Time: 10 minutes | Serving 2 | Difficulty: Easy)

Ingredients:

- 1 + ¼ cup water
- ¼ cup coconut milk
- 1/8 tsp. black pepper
- 1 cup lentils
- Curry Paste
- ¼ teaspoons salt
- Garnishing: Cilantro, lime juice and spring onions

Instructions:

1. In a big saucepan, bring your water to a boil.
2. Add the lentils and constantly stir for 10 minutes while cooking them uncovered. Get rid of the heat.
3. Add additional ingredients and stir. Add salt and fresh herbs as garnish.

Nutritional Info: 222 cal, 4.2g fat (0.6g sag. fat), 0mg chol, 431mg sod, 34g carb (4.5g sugars, 13g fiber), 14g pro.

Frijoles Charros

(Preparation Time: 5 minutes | Cooking Time: 5 minutes | Serving 2 | Difficulty: Easy)

Ingredients:

- 1 garlic clove, chopped
- ¼ pound diced pork
- 2 tomatoes, fresh diced
- ¼ cup cilantro, chopped
- ½ pound pinto beans, dry
- ½ tsp. salt
- ½ chopped onion
- Few jalapeno peppers, sliced

Instructions:

1. Activate the slow cooker and add the precooked pinto beans. Submerge in water. Add salt and garlic mixture.
2. Cook for 5 minutes at high with a cover.
3. At high heat, cook the pork inside a skillet until it is browned. Remove the fat. In the skillet, add the onion until the meat is soft.

Combine tomatoes and jalapenos. Cook until well heated.

4. Add cilantro after serving.

Nutritional Info: 192 cal, 7.1g fat (1.9g sag. fat), 9.9mg chol, 170.6mg sod, 22.2g carb (0.9g sugars, 7.4g fiber), 10.8g pro.

Chickpea Curry

(Preparation Time: 5 minutes | Cooking Time: 10 minutes | Serving 2 | Difficulty: Easy)

Ingredients:

- 2 cups chickpeas, cooked
- Curry Paste
- ½ cup cilantro, chopped

Instructions:

1. Make a paste of curry. Add the chickpeas' liquid to a mixture. Until all the ingredients are well combined, heat and stir as before. Get rid of the heat.

2. Just before serving, add the cilantro, reserving 1 tablespoon for garnish.

Nutritional Info: 257 cal, 7.9g fat (1.1g sag. fat), 0mg chol, 836mg sod, 38g carb (1.7g sugars, 1g fiber), 8.9g pro.

Chapter 3: Salads, Sides and Vegetables Recipes

This chapter includes simple salads, sides and vegetable recipes.

Pecan Chicken Salad

(Preparation Time: 5 minutes | Cooking Time: 0 minutes | Serving 2 | Difficulty: Easy)

Ingredients:

- ¼ cup pecans, chopped
- 2 ribs celery, big diced
- Salt, for taste
- 210 g diced chicken, cooked leftover
- 1/3 cup mayonnaise
- ¼ sweet red onions, medium diced

Instructions:

1. Combine all ingredients and season with salt to taste.
2. Done now!

Nutritional Info: 790 cal, 63g fat (10g sag. fat), 135mg chol, 1550mg sod, 24g carb (15g sugars, 7g fiber), 50g pro.

Spinach Strawberry Salad

(Preparation Time: 15 minutes | Cooking Time: 0 minutes | Serving 2 | Difficulty: Easy)

Ingredients:

- 1 tbsp. poppy seeds
- 1/8 cup lemon juice
- ½ bag spinach, washed, freshly chopped, and dried
- ¼ cup slivered almonds, toasted
- 1 tbsp. black sesame seeds
- ¼ cup cumin or olive oil
- 1/8 tsp. paprika
- 1 cup sliced strawberries

Instructions:

1. Sesame seeds, poppy seeds, olive oil, lemon juice, paprika, and onion are all combined in a bowl. Refrigerate.
2. Combine the strawberries, spinach, and almonds in a big bowl. Dressing over the salad.
3. 15 minutes before serving, toss and place in the fridge.

Nutritional Info: 71 cal, 5.9g fat (1.6g sag. fat), 4.2mg chol, 70mg sod, 3.4g carb (2.1g sugars, 0.9g fiber), 1.9g pro.

Capers and Lemon Tuna Salad

(Preparation Time: 5 minutes | Cooking Time: 0 minutes | Serving 2 | Difficulty: Easy)

Ingredients:

- 2 ribs celery
- 20 g 1/3 cup fresh parsley, chopped
- 1 tablespoon lemon juice
- 142 g 1 tin tuna in olive oil
- 55 g 1/3 cup sweet red onion, diced
- 1 tablespoon capers
- 1 tablespoon mayonnaise

Instructions:

1. Quickly drain the tuna, dice your celery, and add olive oil to the salad.
2. Combine everything else in a large bowl with the addition.

Nutritional Info: 280 cal, 8g fat (2.4g sag. fat), 5mg chol, 0mg sod, 36g carb (9g sugars, 1g fiber), 16g pro.

Cucumber Greek Salad

(Preparation Time: 10 minutes | Cooking Time: 0 minutes | Serving 2 | Difficulty: Easy)

Ingredients:

- 1 teaspoon salt
- ¼ tsp. paprika
- ½ garlic clove, minced
- 1 cup Greek Yogurt, thick
- 2 sliced cucumbers
- 2 tbsp. lemon juice
- ¼ tsp. white pepper
- 2 green onions, freshly diced
- ¼ tsp. paprika

Instructions:

1. Cucumbers should be finely sliced, and then salt should be added. Garlic, white pepper, paprika, lemon juice, and water should be combined and placed away.

2. Slices of cucumber should be squeezed of their moisture one or two at a time and then placed in the dish. Throw away fluids.

3. Add yogurt, green onions, yogurt mixture, and lemon juice. After mixing, top with more dill or paprika.

Nutritional Info: 105.9 cal, 9.5g fat (2.4g sag. fat), 8.3mg chol, 148.8mg sod, 3.9g carb (2.2g sugars, 2.8g fiber), 2g pro.

Caesar Shrimp Salad

(Preparation Time: 5 minutes | Cooking Time: 5 minutes | Serving 2 | Difficulty: Easy)

Ingredients:

- 3 cups torn romaine lettuce
- 2 tablespoons fresh Parmesan cheese
- 10 to 12 cooked shrimp
- 2 tablespoons Caesar dressing, bottled or homemade

Instructions:

1. Start cooking the shrimp for five minutes.

2. While you wait, put your lettuce together, drizzle the dressing onto it, and mix well. Fill your serving platter to the brim.

3. Place the cooked shrimp on top of the lettuce. After sprinkling the Parmesan on top, dig in.

Nutritional Info: 121 cal, 8.1g fat (1.6g sag. fat), 49.7mg chol, 434.1mg sod, 5.6g carb (1g sugars, 1g fiber), 6.5g pro.

Egg Salad

(Preparation Time: 5 minutes | Cooking Time: 7 minutes | Serving 2 | Difficulty: Easy)

Ingredients:

- 1 diced rib of celery
- 5 green olives, chopped and pitted
- Ground black pepper and salt, for taste
- 4 eggs, hard-boiled
- 4 sliced scallions, having crisp green part
- 75 g mayonnaise

Instructions:

1. Cut up your vegetables, peel and finely chop your eggs.

2. Put everything in a large dish and gently toss it to disperse the ingredients while preserving part of the yolk.

3. After adding pepper and salt to taste, the dish is finished.

Nutritional Info: 471 cal, 41g fat (8.7g sag. fat), 523mg chol, 550mg sod, 5.3g carb (2.4g sugars, 1.1g fiber), 18g pro.

Chicken Dilled Salad

(Preparation Time: 10 minutes | Cooking Time: 0 minutes | Serving 2 | Difficulty: Easy)

Ingredients:

- 1 rib celery, large diced
- ¼ sweet red onion, medium diced
- 3 tablespoons sour cream
- Salt, for taste
- 1 ½ cups chicken, cooked diced
- ½ green bell pepper, diced

- 3 tablespoons mayonnaise
- 1 teaspoon dill weed, dried

Instructions:

1. Mix the chicken, green pepper, celery, and onion in a bowl.
2. Combine the mayonnaise, dill, and sour cream, in a separate bowl. Sprinkle salt for taste and serve cooked chicken and vegetables after pouring the sauce over them.

Nutritional Info: 660 cal, 39g fat (6g sag. fat), 135mg chol, 1310mg sod, 30g carb (6g sugars, 4g fiber), 44g pro.

Cauliflower Rice

(Preparation Time: 5 minutes | Cooking Time: 7 minutes | Serving 2 | Difficulty: Easy)

Ingredients:

- ½ head cauliflower
- 1 cup rice, cooked

Instructions:

1. Trim the cauliflower's stems and at the absolute bottom of the stem. Run it through your food processor's shredding blade after cutting it into bits.
2. Inside the microwave, steam for six to seven minutes on high.

Nutritional Info: 25 cal, 0.3g fat (0.1g sag. fat), 0mg chol, 30mg sod, 5g carb (1.9g sugars, 2g fiber), 1.9g pro.

Quinoa Salad

(Preparation Time: 10 minutes | Cooking Time: 2 minutes | Serving 2 | Difficulty: Easy)

Ingredients:

- ½ cup green peas, frozen
- 4 oz. cubed pork
- 1/8 cup almonds, pulsed and crushed
- ½ cup quinoa, cooked
- ¼ cup feta cheese, low-fat
- 1/8 cup cilantro and basil, freshly chopped

Dressing:

- 1/8 cup cumin or olive oil
- 1/8 cup lemon juice
- 1/8 tsp. salt

Instructions:

1. Lower the heat after bringing a pan of water to a boil. Cook the peas till bright green while covered. Pork should be browned in a pan while waiting. Combine the quinoa, pork, feta, peas, herbs, and then almonds in a bowl.
2. Inside a food processor, puree each item for the dressing. Mix the salad ingredients with the dressing. Use a lot of pepper and salt to season. Toss in some new baby spinach before serving.

Nutritional Info: 271 cal, 11g fat (1.5g sag. fat), 0mg chol, 728mg sod, 35g carb (2.5g sugars, 8.6g fiber), 9.2g pro.

Mediterranean Salad

(Preparation Time: 10 minutes | Cooking Time: 0 minutes | Serving 2 | Difficulty: Easy)

Ingredients:

- 1 diced tomato
- ½ green bell pepper, sliced
- 3 thinly sliced radishes
- ¼ cup avocado or olive oil
- 1 clove garlic, minced
- 1 tsp. mint, freshly minced
- 1 head romaine lettuce, small torn
- 1 cucumber, small sliced
- ½ onions, small rings cut
- ¼ cup parsley, flat leaf chopped
- 2 tbsp. lemon juice
- Pepper and salt

Instructions:

1. Add the lettuce, cucumber, tomatoes, pepper, radishes, onion, and parsley inside a salad bowl.

2. Olive oil, garlic, lemon juice, pepper, salt, and mint are all combined in a bowl. Pour over the salad and coat well.

Nutritional Info: 179 cal, 15g fat (5.5g sag. fat), 25mg chol, 370mg sod, 7.4g carb (4.2g sugars, 1.5g fiber), 5.1g pro.

Cucumber, Quinoa, Cilantro Tabbouleh

(Preparation Time: 5 minutes | Cooking Time: 0 minutes | Serving 2 | Difficulty: Easy)

Ingredients:

- ½ cup green pepper and tomato, chopped
- ½ cup cilantro, chopped
- ½ cup quinoa plus 1 tbsp. sesame seeds, cooked
- 1 cup cucumber, chopped

Dressing:

- 1 tbsp. lemon juice, fresh
- 1 pinch of sea salt
- 1 tbsp. avocado or olive oil
- 1 pinch of black pepper

Instructions:

1. Combine all ingredients.

Nutritional Info: 182 cal, 24g fat (0.6g sag. fat), 3mg chol, 259mg sod, 31.6g carb (1.6g sugars, 1.1g fiber), 5g pro.

Sirloin Salad

(Preparation Time: 5 minutes | Cooking Time: 5 minutes | Serving 2 | Difficulty: Easy)

Ingredients:

- 1 cup romaine lettuce, torn
- 2 tablespoons red onion, minced
- ¼ large tomatoes, wedges cut
- 6 ounces sirloin steak, 1 inch thick
- 1 tablespoon vinaigrette
- 2 tablespoons blue cheese, crumbled

Instructions:

1. Place the lettuce on a platter after tossing it with the vinaigrette.
2. Slice the steak medium-thin against the grain after cooking, and then place it on top of the lettuce. Place the tomato wedges over it, then sprinkle the cheese and onion.

Nutritional Info: 490 cal, 26g fat (12g sag. fat), 135mg chol, 1120mg sod, 22g carb (5g sugars, 5g fiber), 45g pro.

Eggs and Cauliflower Salad

(Preparation Time: 5 minutes | Cooking Time: 0 minutes | Serving 2 | Difficulty: Easy)

Ingredients:

- 2 eggs, hard-boiled and chopped
- ½ red onions
- 1 dill pickles
- 1 cup cauliflower, chopped
- 2 oz. cheddar cheese, shredded and low-fat
- 1 celery
- 1 tbsp. yellow mustard

Instructions:

1. Combine all ingredients.

Nutritional Info: 229 cal, 17g fat (3.6g sag. fat), 236mg chol, 546mg sod, 9.4g carb (1.7g sugars, 3.9g fiber), 11g pro.

Caesar Chicken Salad

(Preparation Time: 5 minutes | Cooking Time: 5 minutes | Serving 2 | Difficulty: Easy)

Ingredients:

- 3 cups torn romaine lettuce
- 2 tablespoons Parmesan cheese, fresh
- 6 ounces of skinless and boneless chicken breast
- 2 tablespoons Caesar dressing, bottled or homemade

Instructions:

1. Start grilling the chicken breast for around 5 minutes; if you'd like, you may also sauté it.

2. While you wait, put your lettuce together, drizzle the dressing across it, and mix well. Fill your serving platter to the brim.

3. Slice the cooked chicken breast into thin strips, and then arrange them on top of the lettuce. After sprinkling the Parmesan on top, dig in.

Nutritional Info: 130 cal, 8.6g fat (1.8g sag. fat), 22.4mg chol, 252.8mg sod, 5.3g carb (1g sugars, 1g fiber), 7.7g pro.

Fried Japanese Rice

(Preparation Time: 6 minutes | Cooking Time: 9 minutes | Serving 2 | Difficulty: Easy)

Ingredients:

- 2 eggs
- 2 tablespoons butter
- 2 tablespoons carrot, shredded
- Ground black pepper and salt, for taste
- ½ head cauliflower
- 1 cup snow pea pods, fresh
- ½ cup onion, diced
- 3 tablespoons soy sauce
- 1 cup rice, cooked

Instructions:

1. The eggs should be whisked before being added to a nonstick pan and heated over medium-high heat. Use the spatula to smash the eggs into pea-sized pieces while they cook. Take out of the skillet, and then put it aside.

2. The snow peas should be de-tipped and strung before being cut into 1/4-inch lengths.

3. Pea pods, carrots, and onion should be sautéed for two to three minutes in melted butter in a pan. After thoroughly combining everything, add the cauliflower. Soy sauce is added, and the mixture is cooked for five to six minutes while frequently stirring. Serve with a little salt and pepper.

Nutritional Info: 253 cal, 9.4g fat (1.4g sag. fat), 94mg chol, 410mg sod, 31g carb (2.7g sugars, 2g fiber), 11g pro.

Avocado Pomegranate Salad

(Preparation Time: 5 minutes | Cooking Time: 0 minutes | Serving 2 | Difficulty: Easy)

Ingredients:

- 1 ripe avocado, ½ inch pieces cut
- ½ cup pecan
- ½ cup cherry tomatoes
- 2 cups mixed greens, arugula, spinach, red leaf lettuce
- 1 cup pomegranate seeds
- ½ cup blackberries
- Olive oil, lemon juice, salt

Instructions:

1. In a salad dish, combine the greens, diced tomatoes, avocado, pecan, pomegranates, and blackberries.

2. Pour over the salad after combining olive oil, salt, and lemon juice in a bowl.

Nutritional Info: 316 cal, 18g fat (2g sag. fat), 0mg chol, 24mg sod, 36g carb (8g sugars, 9g fiber), 7g pro.

Broccoli Cheddar Salad

(Preparation Time: 5 minutes | Cooking Time: 0 minutes | Serving 2 | Difficulty: Easy)

Ingredients:

- 1 ½ cups Cheddar cheese, shredded
- 1 ½ cups mayonnaise
- 3 tablespoons cider or red wine vinegar
- 6 cups broccoli florets, fresh
- 1/3 cup onion, chopped
- 12-18g Splenda
- 12 slices bacon, crumbled and cooked

Instructions:

1. Combine the cheese, broccoli, and onion in a big bowl. Mayonnaise, Splenda, and vinegar should be combined; pour the

mixture over broccoli, then toss to coat. Place in the fridge for a minimum of 4 hours. Put the bacon in just before serving.

2. If you'd like, you may softly cook the broccoli, let it cool, and then mix in the other components. Avoid going past tender-crisp, however.

Nutritional Info: 260 cal, 22.9g fat (3.4g sag. fat), 10mg chol, 336mg sod, 9g carb (4g sugars, 1g fiber), 3.9g pro.

Almond-Chicken Noodle Salad

(Preparation Time: 5 minutes | Cooking Time: 5 minutes | Serving 2 | Difficulty: Easy)

Ingredients:

- 3 tablespoons almonds, slivered
- 2 tablespoons mayonnaise
- 2 teaspoons soy sauce
- 6 drops Sriracha
- 2 scallions
- 225 g 1 package tofu shirataki, width fettuccine
- 1 ½ teaspoons coconut oil
- 1 tablespoon almond butter
- ½ teaspoon fresh ginger root, grated
- ½ cup chicken, cooked

Instructions:

1. Open the tofu shirataki package with a knife, and then pour the contents into a strainer inside the sink. Since they are so long, rinse them thoroughly and cut them in half with your kitchen shears.

2. Shirataki should be placed in a microwave-safe bowl and heated for two minutes. Drain one more, then repeat the process two more times.

3. While you finish the remainder, let them cool.

4. Start frying your nuts in the coconut oil in a small, sturdy pan over medium heat.

5. In a modest dish, combine the mayonnaise, soy sauce, nut butter, Sriracha and ginger root. You should dress like this.

6. Return and stir your almonds! Mix them once before spooning out portions of the dressing. Don't let them burn, please. Remove them from off fire as soon as they begin to get golden.

7. Chicken should be cut into 1/2-inch pieces. Scallions should be thinly sliced, including the fresh green portion.

8. It's time to put your salad together now. Put the shirataki in a bowl for mixing.

9. Add the dressing, followed by the scallions, chicken, and toasted almonds. After a quick stir, you're done!

Nutritional Info: 299 cal, 16g fat (3g sag. fat), 21mg chol, 168mg sod, 16g carb (6g sugars, 1g fiber), 5g pro.

Quinoa, Asparagus, Red Peppers Salad

(Preparation Time: 5 minutes | Cooking Time: 0 minutes | Serving 2 | Difficulty: Easy)

Ingredients:

- 1 cup red peppers, sliced
- Garnish with parsley and lime
- ½ cup quinoa plus 1 tbsp. sunflower seeds, cooked
- 1 cup asparagus, grilled

Dressing:

- 1 tbsp. lemon juice, fresh
- 1 pinch of sea salt
- 1 tbsp. avocado or olive oil
- 1 pinch of black pepper

Instructions:

1. Combine all ingredients.

Nutritional Info: 355 cal, 13g fat (1.5g sag. fat), 3mg chol, 488mg sod, 48g carb (9g sugars, 7g fiber), 12g pro.

Tuna Salad

(Preparation Time: 5 minutes | Cooking Time: 0 minutes | Serving 2 | Difficulty: Easy)

Ingredients:

- ½ green bell pepper
- 5 ounces 1 tin tuna in olive oil
- 30 g 2 tablespoons minced bread plus butter pickles, sugar-free
- 2 ribs celery, big or small, 3
- ¼ sweet red onion, medium
- 1/3 cup mayonnaise

Instructions:

1. The veggies are into dice. It is between 1 ½ and 2 cups of vegetables!

2. The mayonnaise, tuna, and pickles are then combined. I've been tempted to eat this directly from the mixing bowl.

Nutritional Info: 383 cal, 23.3g fat (12.3g sag. fat), 43.7mg chol, 807mg sod, 14.1g carb (10.5g sugars, 0.8g fiber), 29.7g pro.

Club Sandwich Salad

(Preparation Time: 5 minutes | Cooking Time: 5 minutes | Serving 2 | Difficulty: Easy)

Ingredients:

- 2 cups diced turkey, cooked
- 1 tomato, large diced
- 2 tablespoons cider vinegar
- 1 teaspoon spicy brown mustard
- Ground black pepper and salt, for taste
- ½ head cauliflower
- 1 heart romaine lettuce, ½ inch strips
- ½ cup mayonnaise
- 2 tablespoons lemon juice
- 10 bacon, cooked crisp slices

Instructions:

1. Your half-head of cauliflower should have removed the leaves and the very bottom of the stem. Chop it up, and then process it in your food processor using the shredding blade. The finished "rice" should be placed in a microwave-safe casserole dish using a cover and some water and heat on high for about 6 minutes.

2. Put the lettuce, turkey, and tomato inside a large salad dish.

3. Pull out your cauliflower rice & uncover it when the microwave beeps to halt the cooking process. So that it won't cook the lettuce and tomatoes, give it a few minutes to cool. If I drain it and stir it sometimes, it will cool down more quickly.

4. Your mayonnaise, lemon juice, vinegar, and mustard should be measured and whisked together.

5. Cut your bacon into the salad with your kitchen shears, about every 1/4 inch. The cauliflower rice is added, followed by the dressing, pepper and salt to taste, toss, and serve.

Nutritional Info: 250 cal, 11g fat (4g sag. fat), 5mg chol, 210mg sod, 30g carb (16g sugars, 11g fiber), 9g pro.

Chili Cheese Chicken Salad

(Preparation Time: 5 minutes | Cooking Time: 7 minutes | Serving 2 | Difficulty: Moderate)

Ingredients:

- 1 cup celery, diced
- 1/3 cup diced red onion, diced
- 2 cups cooked chicken, diced
- 1/3 cup mayonnaise
- 1 ½ teaspoons lime juice
- ½ teaspoon cumin, ground
- 2 ounces black olives, drained slices
- ½ head cauliflower
- ½ diced red bell pepper
- ¼ cup green chiles, diced
- 4 ounces Monterey Jack cheese, ¼ inch cubes cut
- 1 tablespoon white vinegar
- 1 teaspoon chili powder
- ½ teaspoon oregano, dried

Instructions:

1. Cauliflower should first be chopped into 1 ½ inch pieces. Please put it in a casserole dish having a lid that can be microwaved, add a few teaspoons of water, cover it, and cook it for 7 minutes on high.

2. Build your other chicken, vegetables, and cheese in a large mixing bowl while that's cooking.

3. Pull your cauliflower out of the microwave, expose it, and drain it. Give it some time to settle and cool. You don't want your cheese to melt. If you stir the cauliflower occasionally, it will cool down more quickly.

4. Measure out your mayonnaise, lime juice, vinegar, cumin, chili powder, and oregano as you wait for the cauliflower to cool. Mix everything.

5. Okay, has the cauliflower somewhat cooled off? Add and toss it around with the cheese, chicken, and vegetables. Place the olives within, add the dressing, and toss to combine. You may consume this immediately.

Nutritional Info: 250 cal, 11g fat (4g sag. fat), 5mg chol, 210mg sod, 30g carb (16g sugars, 11g fiber), 9g pro.

Mushroom Risotto

(Preparation Time: 5 minutes | Cooking Time: 8 minutes | Serving 2 | Difficulty: Easy)

Ingredients:

- 3 tablespoons butter
- ½ onions, medium diced
- 2 tablespoons dry vermouth
- ¾ cup Parmesan cheese, grated
- 2 tablespoons parsley, freshly chopped
- ½ head cauliflower
- 1 cup mushrooms, sliced
- 1 teaspoon or 2 cloves garlic, minced
- 1 tablespoon chicken bouillon concentrate
- Xanthan or guar, as required

Instructions:

1. Melt your butter in a large pan over medium-high heat while the cauliflower cooks. Combine the onion, mushrooms, and garlic in the pan while sautéing.

2. Drain the cauliflower off the microwave after its finished cooking. Add your cauliflower to the pan and toss everything together after the mushrooms have changed color and seem to be done. Vermouth and bouillon are stirred in, followed by the cheese, and the mixture is cooked for 2 to 3 minutes.

3. To make the "risotto" a creamy texture, sprinkle xanthan or guar over it with a little amount while swirling constantly. Just before serving, stir in the parsley.

Nutritional Info: 243 cal, 9.8g fat (3g sag. fat), 16mg chol, 268mg sod, 30g carb (4g sugars, 1g fiber), 7.6g pro.

Almond Chicken Rice

(Preparation Time: 5 minutes | Cooking Time: 5 minutes | Serving 2 | Difficulty: Easy)

Ingredients:

- ½ chopped medium onion
- ¼ cup dry white wine
- 1 teaspoon poultry seasoning
- ½ head cauliflower
- 2 tablespoons divided butter
- 1 tablespoon chicken bouillon concentrate
- ¼ cup almonds, slivered or sliced

Instructions:

1. Over medium-high heat, sauté your onion with 1 tablespoon of butter in a big, heavy pan.

2. Drain the cauliflower out of the microwave after its finished cooking, and then add it to the pan with the onion. Stir in the wine, poultry spice, and chicken bouillon concentrate. Lower the temperature.

3. Once you sauté your almonds in the final tablespoon of butter inside a small, heavy pan, let it simmer for a few minutes. Stir the almonds into the "rice" until they have become golden, and then serve.

Nutritional Info: 267 cal, 6g fat (1g sag. fat), 66mg chol, 465mg sod, 23g carb (1.2g sugars, 2.6g fiber), 31g pro.

Little Mama's Side Dish

(Preparation Time: 5 minutes | Cooking Time: 5 minutes | Serving 2 | Difficulty: Easy)

Ingredients:

- ½ head cauliflower
- ½ onion, medium
- 4 slices bacon
- ½ green bell pepper
- ¼ cup stuffed olives, sliced

Instructions:

1. Start cooking the bacon in a big, heavy pan over medium-high heat after chopping it into tiny pieces.

2. Cauliflower should be cut into 1/2-inch pieces. Rather than waste it, chop up its stem as well. Put your chopped cauliflower inside a microwave-safe casserole dish with a lid or, if you have one, a microwave steamer. Cover, cook for 8 minutes on high, and remove from the microwave.

3. Return to the cutting board after stirring the bacon. Slice the onion and pepper. The bacon is now beginning to brown on the edges and has lost some grease. To the skillet, add the onion and pepper. Sauté until the pepper begins to soften and the onion becomes transparent.

4. The cauliflower ought to should be finished by then. The additional tiny amount of water will assist in dissolving the delicious bacon taste from the bottom of the pan and convey it through the dish. Add to the skillet despite draining and mix.

5. Add the olives, stir, and simmer for one additional minute before serving.

Nutritional Info: 49 cal, 4g fat (2g sag. fat), 5mg chol, 210mg sod, 3g carb (1g sugars, 0g fiber), 2g pro.

Bacon and Beef Rice With Pine Nuts

(Preparation Time: 5 minutes | Cooking Time: 15 minutes | Serving 2 | Difficulty: Easy)

Ingredients:

- 4 strips bacon
- 2 tablespoons tomato sauce
- 2 tablespoons pine nuts, toasted
- ½ head cauliflower
- ½ onions, medium chopped
- 1 tablespoon beef bouillon concentrates
- 2 tablespoons fresh parsley, chopped

Instructions:

1. Cut the bacon into small pieces while it cooks; kitchen shears work well. Then, fry the bacon bits in a large pan over medium-high heat. Add the onion to the pan after the bacon has released some of its oil. Cook until the bacon is crisp and browned and the onion is transparent.

2. The cauliflower ought to be finished by now. It is drained and added to the pan along with the onion and bacon. You may add a few tablespoons of water if you wish to assist the liquid flavorings spread. Add your tomato sauce with beef bouillon concentrate, and whisk everything together.

3. Serve after adding the parsley and pine nuts.

Nutritional Info: 344 cal, 16g fat (4g sag. fat), 5mg chol, 10mg sod, 30g carb (1g sugars, 1g fiber), 18g pro.

Hazelnut Green Beans

(Preparation Time: 5 minutes | Cooking Time: 10 minutes | Serving 2 | Difficulty: Easy)

Ingredients:

- ¼ cup hazelnuts
- 2 tablespoons lemon juice
- 1 pound green beans, frozen
- 2 tablespoons olive oil
- Ground black pepper and salt, for taste

Instructions:

1. Green beans should be placed in a microwave-safe casserole dish using a little cover of water and microwaved on high for about 7 minutes.

2. It will help if you cut your hazelnuts in the meanwhile. When the hazelnuts are golden and fragrant, add olive oil to a large, heavy skillet and set it over medium heat. Get rid of the heat.

3. The microwave has now started to beep. Give your beans another three to four minutes after stirring them.

4. Drain the beans once they are crisp-tender, then return them to the pan with the lemon juice. Serve after tossing everything together and adding pepper and salt to taste.

Nutritional Info: 140 cal, 12g fat (4g sag. fat), 0mg chol, 45mg sod, 8g carb (5g sugars, 3g fiber), 3g pro.

Pineapple Curried Rice

(Preparation Time: 5 minutes | Cooking Time: 5 minutes | Serving 2 | Difficulty: Easy)

Ingredients:

- 2 tbsp. margarine or butter
- 2 minced garlic cloves
- 5 cups chicken broth
- 1 tbsp. soy sauce
- 20 oz. 1 tin pineapple chunks, unsweetened drained
- ½ cup onion, finely chopped
- 2 ½ cups long grain rice, uncooked
- 1 tbsp. curry powder
- 1 jalapeno pepper, chopped and seeded (optional)
- 4 chopped green onions

Instructions:

1. Cook onion in butter in a big pot until it's soft. Add the rice, curry powder, and garlic. If desired, add broth, soy sauce, and jalapenos to boil. For twenty minutes, simmer with the heat down and the lid on.

2. As soon as the liquid has been absorbed, take it off the stove and sit for five minutes.

3. Add pineapple chunks and green onions after mixing.

Nutritional Info: 178 cal, 3g fat (2g sag. fat), 1mg chol, 96mg sod, 34g carb (16g sugars, 9g fiber), 4g pro.

Mushrooms with Sun-Dried Tomatoes, Bacon, and Cheese

(Preparation Time: 5 minutes | Cooking Time: 10 minutes | Serving 2 | Difficulty: Easy)

Ingredients:

- 8 ounces mushrooms, sliced
- ¼ cup sun-dried tomatoes, diced
- 1/3 cup Parmesan cheese, shredded
- 4 slices bacon
- ½ teaspoon garlic, minced
- 2 tablespoons heavy cream

Instructions:

1. The bacon should be chopped or chopped with kitchen shears. It should be prepared in a large, heavy skillet over high heat. Stir inside the mushrooms as part of the bacon's oil is rendered.

2. The mushrooms should be cooked until they begin to soften and change color. Add the garlic, stir, and simmer for 4 to 5 minutes. Once the cream has been absorbed, stir in the tomatoes.

3. Spread the cheese evenly over the mixture, mix it in, and then finish cooking it for one more minute before serving.

Nutritional Info: 120 cal, 11g fat (1g sag. fat), 3mg chol, 65mg sod, 5g carb (3g sugars, 2g fiber), 1g pro.

Lemon Chicken with Rice

(Preparation Time: 5 minutes | Cooking Time: 9 minutes | Serving 2 | Difficulty: Easy)

Ingredients:

- 1 onion, medium chopped
- 2 minced garlic cloves
- 2 tbsp. cornstarch
- 2 tbsp. lemon juice
- 1 ½ cups instant rice, uncooked
- 1 lb. chicken breasts, skinless and boneless strips cut
- 1 large thinly sliced carrot
- 2 tbsp. margarine or butter
- 14 ½ oz. 1 tin chicken broth
- ½ tsp. salt
- 1 cup peas, frozen

Instructions:

1. The ingredients should be cooked in butter in a pan for five to seven minutes or until the chicken is no pinker. Combine the cornflour, broth, lemon juice, and optional salt in a bowl and whisk until smooth. Add in skillet and heat through.

2. Cook and stir until thickened, about 2 minutes. Relish on rice and peas. Please turn off the heat, cover the pan, and let it stand for five minutes.

Nutritional Info: 235 cal, 5g fat (4g sag. fat), 43mg chol, 156mg sod, 27g carb (14g sugars, 9g fiber), 20g pro.

Cauliflower Two-Cheese

(Preparation Time: 5 minutes | Cooking Time: 12 minutes | Serving 2 | Difficulty: Easy)

Ingredients:

- 1 egg, large
- 1 cup sour cream
- 1/8 teaspoon black pepper, ground
- Optional: 2 tablespoons fresh parsley, chopped
- 1 head cauliflower, florets cut

- 1 cup cottage cheese, whole-milk
- ½ teaspoon salt
- 8 ounces sharp Cheddar cheese, shredded

Instructions:

1. Set the oven to 350°F. Spray some nonstick cooking spray lightly in a 2-quart baking dish.

2. In a microwave-safe casserole dish, add the cauliflower florets and two tablespoons of water, then cover. It should be quite tender after ten to eleven minutes in the microwave.

3. Before baking, mix 2 teaspoons of the poppy seeds into the cauliflower. It provides a sort of polka-dot appearance and elevates the taste with a subdued refinement.

Nutritional Info: 237 cal, 15g fat (8g sag. fat), 41mg chol, 252mg sod, 17g carb (4g sugars, 3g fiber), 11g pro.

Cumin Mushrooms

(Preparation Time: 5 minutes | Cooking Time: 5 minutes | Serving 2 | Difficulty: Easy)

Ingredients:

- 1 ½ tablespoons butter
- 1 teaspoon cumin, ground
- 2 tablespoons sour cream
- 8 ounces mushrooms, sliced
- 1 ½ tablespoons olive oil
- ¼ teaspoon black pepper, ground

Instructions:

1. Over medium-high heat, begin sautéing the mushrooms inside the butter and oil.

2. Add the pepper and cumin once they have become limp and changed color. After a few minutes of cooking time with the seasonings, add the sour cream to the mushrooms. Just enough even to bring to a boil before serving.

Nutritional Info: 8 cal, 1g fat (0.4g sag. fat), 4mg chol, 21mg sod, 1g carb (0.6g sugars, 0.1g fiber), 0.3g pro.

Balsamic Green Beans with Pine Nuts and Bacon

(Preparation Time: 5 minutes | Cooking Time: 5 minutes | Serving 2 | Difficulty: Easy)

Ingredients:

- 1 pound green beans, frozen
- 1 tablespoon olive oil
- 1 teaspoon marjoram, dried
- 2 tablespoons balsamic vinegar
- ¼ medium onions
- 1 teaspoon butter
- ¼ cup pine nuts, toasted
- 2 slices bacon

Instructions:

1. The bacon should be placed in a glass pie dish or on a heated bacon rack. To make it crisp, microwave it for two min on high. Drain then set aside after removing from the microwave.

2. Put the green beans, already frozen, in a microwave-safe casserole dish under a cover while the bacon cooks. Whenever the bacon is cooked, add a few tablespoons of water, cover, and microwave for 7 minutes on high.

3. You want to finely mince the onion, so chop it up. Put your large skillet over medium heat, spray it with nonstick cooking spray, and then add the butter and olive oil. Stir the melted butter into olive oil before adding the onion.

4. The onion should be transparent after just several minutes of sautéing. Add the marjoram and stir.

5. Turn off the heat if the beans aren't done yet; it's safer than burning your onion!

6. Green beans should be stirred and given three additional minutes after the microwave whistles. They must be cooked just enough to be soft.

Nutritional Info: 75 cal, 2.6g fat (0.5g sag. fat), 10mg chol, 50mg sod, 11g carb (1g sugars, 1g fiber), 3.4g pro.

Broccoli Chicken

(Preparation Time: 5 minutes | Cooking Time: 20 minutes | Serving 2 | Difficulty: Easy)

Ingredients:

- 10 oz. chicken, boneless and skinless
- Salt and pepper
- 1 cup Yogurt Dressing
- 4 tbsp. grated cheddar cheese, low-fat
- 2 cups broccoli florets
- 2 tsp. flax seeds meal
- 2 beaten eggs
- ½ cup chicken broth

Instructions:

1. Preheat oven to 400 degrees. Give broccoli around 5 minutes to cook. Chicken is added, broccoli is removed, and 15 minutes are simmered. Chicken that has been cubed should be combined with broccoli.

2. Combine the flax, salt, and pepper in a skillet with the liquid. High heat, boil and simmer for one minute while stirring continuously. Get rid of the heat. Stirring until well blended, add the yogurt dressing, beaten egg, and half of the cheese.

3. The mixture of broccoli and sauce will be blended after adding the sauce.

4. Please fill the casserole dish with the ingredients and coat it with little coconut oil. Sprinkle the remaining cheese over the top.

Nutritional Info: 219 cal, 12g fat (1g sag. fat), 39mg chol, 508mg sod, 14g carb (5g sugars, 2g fiber), 15g pro.

Pesto Gorgonzola Caesar Salad

(Preparation Time: 5 minutes | Cooking Time: 0 minutes | Serving 2 | Difficulty: Easy)

Ingredients:

- 3 tablespoons olive oil, extra-virgin
- 1/3 cup Gorgonzola cheese, crumbled
- 6 cups romaine lettuce hearts, torn
- 1 ½ tablespoons pesto sauce

Instructions:

1. In a large salad dish, place your lettuce. Pesto and olive oil should be combined before being poured over the salad and vigorously mixed to cover everything. Add the Gorgonzola, give everything one more gentle toss, and serve.

Nutritional Info: 340 cal, 33g fat (8g sag. fat), 20mg chol, 856mg sod, 6g carb (1g sugars, 3g fiber), 7g pro.

Cuke and Sour Cream Salad

(Preparation Time: 5 minutes | Cooking Time: 5 minutes | Serving 2 | Difficulty: Easy)

Ingredients:

- 1 green bell pepper
- ½ head cauliflower
- 1 cup sour cream
- 2 teaspoons dill weed, dried
- 2 cucumbers, scrubbed
- ½ large red onion, sweet
- 2 teaspoons salt
- 2 tablespoons vinegar

Instructions:

1. As evenly as possible, slice the cauliflower, onion, pepper, and cucumber. Although a food processor's slicing blade saves a lot of time, I've also cut things using a good paring knife.

2. The veggies should be well-salted before being chilled for a couple of hours in the fridge.

3. Mix the vinegar, sour cream, and dill well in a separate basin.

4. After taking the vegetables out of the refrigerator and draining any water accumulated at the bottom of your bowl, incorporate the sour cream combination. Before serving, place in the fridge for at least a few hours.

Nutritional Info: 93 cal, 6g fat (3g sag. fat), 20mg chol, 722mg sod, 6g carb (4g sugars, 0g fiber), 1g pro.

Spinach Classic Salad

(Preparation Time: 5 minutes | Cooking Time: 0 minutes | Serving 2 | Difficulty: Easy)

Ingredients:

- 1/8 sweet red onion, large, thinly sliced
- 2 tablespoons cider vinegar
- 9 drops liquid stevia
- 1/8 teaspoon dry mustard
- 2 slices bacon, cooked, crumbled and crisp
- 4 cups spinach, fresh
- 3 tablespoons oil
- 2 teaspoons tomato paste
- ¼ small onion, grated
- Ground black pepper and salt, for taste
- 1 egg, hard-boiled chopped

Instructions:

1. Dry off the spinach after a thorough wash. Rip up the bigger leaves. Combine in a salad dish with the onion.

2. Combine the oil, tomato paste, vinegar, Stevia, mustard, grated red onion, pepper and salt to taste in a separate bowl. Toss the onion and spinach after adding the mixture to them.

3. Add bacon and an egg to each plate.

Nutritional Info: 134 cal, 10g fat (3g sag. fat), 63mg chol, 247mg sod, 3g carb (1g sugars, 0g fiber), 6g pro.

Southwestern Salad

(Preparation Time: 5 minutes | Cooking Time: 5 minutes | Serving 2 | Difficulty: Easy)

Ingredients:

- ½ cup mayonnaise
- 1 tablespoon lime juice
- 1/3 cup chopped fresh cilantro
- 1 clove crushed garlic
- ½ head cauliflower
- 2 tablespoons spicy mustard
- 1 small jalapeño
- 1/3 cup red onion, diced
- 1 tomato, small

Instructions:

1. Cauliflower should first be chopped into 1/2-inch pieces. The core should be removed along with the remainder of the cauliflower. Put some water and the cauliflower pieces in a microwave-safe casserole dish using a cover, and heat for 7 minutes on high.

2. Drain the cooked cauliflower and place it in a wide mixing basin. Mayonnaise, lime juice, and mustard should be combined in a medium bowl before mixing with the cauliflower.

3. Remove the seeds from the jalapeño, and then finely chop the fruit. After adding it, combine it with the salad's onion, cilantro, and garlic.

4. Last but not least, remove the tomato's stem and chop it into the smallest chunks before delicately incorporating it. Before serving, let the salad chill for a few hours.

Nutritional Info: 131 cal, 6g fat (1g sag. fat), 5mg chol, 230mg sod, 16g carb (2g sugars, 3g fiber), 4g pro.

Asparagus Sesame Salad

(Preparation Time: 5 minutes | Cooking Time: 4 minutes | Serving 2 | Difficulty: Easy)

Ingredients:

- 4 teaspoons soy sauce
- 1 tablespoon sesame seeds
- 1 pound asparagus
- 2 teaspoons sesame oil, dark

Instructions:

1. Asparagus should be cut where they naturally desire to break. Put the spears in a microwave-safe casserole dish or steamer with a cover after cutting them into 1 1/2-inch length. In either case, cover with a few tablespoons of water and microwave for 3–4 minutes.

2. As quickly as the microwave sounds, cover your asparagus to finish cooking it. Drain well, and then place in a long, thin bowl.

3. Sesame oil and soy sauce should be combined. Add the asparagus to the mixture and stir. For one hour or two, relax.

4. When ready to serve, place the sesame seeds inside a small, clean skillet over medium-low heat. Shake the pan occasionally until the sesame seeds begin to hop about and emit a toasted aroma. Get rid of the heat. Serve the asparagus immediately after adding the sesame seeds.

Nutritional Info: 48 cal, 2g fat (1g sag. fat), 0mg chol, 68mg sod, 6g carb (2g sugars, 1g fiber), 3g pro.

Tossed Favorite Salad

(Preparation Time: 10 minutes | Cooking Time: 0 minutes | Serving 2 | Difficulty: Easy)

Ingredients:

- ½ cup olive oil, extra-virgin
- ½ cup fresh parsley, chopped
- ¼ cucumber, sliced and quartered
- 2 to 3 tablespoons of lemon juice
- ¼ cup Parmesan cheese, grated
- 1 clove garlic
- 1 head romaine lettuce
- ½ green diced bell pepper
- ¼ sweet red onion, thinly sliced
- 2 to 3 teaspoons Worcestershire sauce
- 1 ripe tomato, medium thin wedges cut

Instructions:

1. C crushes the garlic clove in a small dish and then pours the olive oil. Set the bowl aside.

2. Your romaine should be cleaned, dried, and broken up. Add the parsley, cucumber, pepper, and onion to this mixture. The salad should be coated with garlic-flavored oil after drizzling over it.

3. Add lemon juice to taste, and then mix one more. After that, add as much Worcestershire sauce as you want and mix once more. Add the Parmesan last, then give everything one final toss. Serve the dish with tomato wedges on top.

Nutritional Info: 148 cal, 13g fat (3g sag. fat), 9mg chol, 176mg sod, 6g carb (3g sugars, 2g fiber), 3g pro.

Plum Spinach Salad

(Preparation Time: 5 minutes | Cooking Time: 0 minutes | Serving 2 | Difficulty: Easy)

Ingredients:

- 2 red plums
- 2 tablespoons light olive oil, peanut oil, or MCT oil
- 1 teaspoon soy sauce
- 3 drops liquid stevia
- 12 cups baby spinach
- 2 sliced scallions
- 2 tablespoons rice vinegar
- ½ teaspoon fresh ginger root, grated

Instructions:

1. Put your large salad dish full of baby spinach.

2. After being halved, the plums should be cut into ½ inch cubes and the pits removed. Slice your onions, paying attention to the crisp green portion.

3. Mix the peanut oil, soy sauce, rice vinegar, ginger, and stevia in a small bowl. When the spinach is well covered with the dressing, pour this over it.

4. Place the spinach on Individual salad plates; add plum cubes and scallions to each dish, and then plate.

Nutritional Info: 157 cal, 5g fat (4g sag. fat), 2mg chol, 377mg sod, 23g carb (16g sugars, 11g fiber), 5g pro.

Tomato, Bacon, and Cauliflower Salad

(Preparation Time: 5 minutes | Cooking Time: 0 minutes | Serving 2 | Difficulty: Easy)

Ingredients:

- 8 ounces of bacon, cooked, crumbled and crisp
- 10 scallions, sliced
- Ground black pepper and salt, for taste
- ½ head cauliflower
- 1 tomato, large chopped
- ½ cup mayonnaise
- Optional: Lettuce

Instructions:

1. Use the shredding disc in a food processor to process the cauliflower. It should be microwaved or steamed until tender-crisp.

2. In a large bowl, combine the cooked cauliflower, tomato, bacon, scallions, &

mayonnaise. Mix with pepper and salt to taste.

3. If desired, you may compress this salad into a custard cup and then unmold it into a dish covered with lettuce; it looks lovely. This salad keeps a molded form well.

Nutritional Info: 428 cal, 36g fat (8g sag. fat), 32mg chol, 495mg sod, 16g carb (10g sugars, 2g fiber), 9g pro.

Mixed Greens with Goat Cheese, Walnuts, and Raspberry Dressing

(Preparation Time: 5 minutes | Cooking Time: 0 minutes | Serving 2 | Difficulty: Easy)

Ingredients:

- 4 cups leaf lettuce, torn
- 2 cups radicchio, torn
- 3 tablespoons walnuts, chopped
- 4 cups romaine lettuce, torn
- 2 cups arugula, torn
- 2 ounces of goat cheese
- ½ cup Raspberry Vinaigrette

Instructions:

1. In your salad bowl, combine the arugula, lettuce, and radicchio. Your goat cheese should be cut into little chunks. Have your walnuts prepared and chopped?

2. Then, after adding the dressing to the greens, toss. Place the salad on five plates, and then garnish each with raspberries, walnuts, and goat cheese.

Nutritional Info: 195 cal, 17g fat (3g sag. fat), 2mg chol, 94mg sod, 10g carb (3g sugars, 1g fiber), 4g pro.

French Vinaigrette

(Preparation Time: 2 minutes | Cooking Time: 0 minutes | Serving 2 | Difficulty: Easy)

Ingredients:

- 1/3 cup wine vinegar
- 1 crushed clove garlic

- ¼ teaspoon black pepper, ground
- ¾ cup olive oil, extra-virgin
- 1 teaspoon Dijon mustard
- ½ teaspoon salt

Instructions:

1. Combine everything in a clean container, secure the top, and shake briskly. You may shake it again immediately before using it after storing it in the jar.

Nutritional Info: 120 cal, 11g fat (4g sag. fat), 6mg chol, 250mg sod, 5g carb (3g sugars, 0g fiber), 0g pro.

Sour and Sweet Cabbage

(Preparation Time: 5 minutes | Cooking Time: 10 minutes | Serving 2 | Difficulty: Easy)

Ingredients:

- 4 cups cabbage, shredded
- 12 drops liquid stevia
- 3 slices bacon
- 2 tablespoons cider vinegar

Instructions:

1. The bacon should be cooked until crisp in a large pan. Drain and remove.

2. In the bacon fat, add the cabbage and sauté for 10 minutes or until it is tender-crisp.

3. The stevia and vinegar should be combined. Add this to the cabbage and stir. Just before serving, include the crumbled bacon to keep it crisp.

Nutritional Info: 138 cal, 6g fat (4g sag. fat), 18mg chol, 261mg sod, 19g carb (14g sugars, 3g fiber), 2g pro.

Italian Vinaigrette

(Preparation Time: 2 minutes | Cooking Time: 0 minutes | Serving 2 | Difficulty: Easy)

Ingredients:

- 1/3 cup wine vinegar
- ½ teaspoon oregano, dried
- ¼ teaspoon black pepper, ground

- 2 crushed cloves of garlic
- 2/3 cup olive oil, extra-virgin
- ½ teaspoon salt
- ¼ teaspoon basil, dried
- 1 mini pinch of red pepper flakes

Instructions:

1. Put everything in a jar, secure the top, and shake, shake, shake. Mix it once more before using it after keeping it in the refrigerator in the jar.

Nutritional Info: 35 cal, 3g fat (1g sag. fat), 0mg chol, 140mg sod, 1g carb (1g sugars, 0g fiber), 0.1g pro.

Asparagus along with Curried Walnut Butter

(Preparation Time: 5 minutes | Cooking Time: 5 minutes | Serving 2 | Difficulty: Easy)

Ingredients:

- ¼ cup butter
- 1 teaspoon curry powder
- 9 drops liquid stevia
- 1 pound asparagus
- 2 tablespoons walnuts, chopped
- ½ teaspoon cumin, ground

Instructions:

1. Asparagus should be cut off where they naturally desire to break. You may use a glass pie dish and plastic wrap or place it in a microwave-safe container with a cover.

2. In each case, add one or two tablespoons of water and cover.

3. 5 minutes on high in the microwave. Don't forget to uncover the asparagus as soon as the microwave beeps; otherwise, it will continue to cook and become limp.

4. Place the butter inside a medium pan over medium heat while heating.

5. Put the walnuts in when it has melted. Until they are toasted, stir them for two to three minutes. After adding the cumin, curry

powder, and stevia, stir for another two minutes.

6. Your asparagus is now finished. With tongs, please remove it from the container, place it on the serving plates, and then drizzle your curried walnut butter on top.

Nutritional Info: 67 cal, 5g fat (2g sag. fat), 5mg chol, 161mg sod, 6g carb (1g sugars, 2g fiber), 3g pro.

Dragon's Teeth

(Preparation Time: 5 minutes | Cooking Time: 8 minutes | Serving 2 | Difficulty: Easy)

Ingredients:

- ¼ cup chili garlic paste
- 2 teaspoons sesame oil, dark
- 12 drops stevia, liquid
- 2 teaspoons rice vinegar
- 1 head Napa cabbage
- 2 tablespoons soy sauce
- 1 teaspoon salt
- 2 tablespoons canola or peanut oil

Instructions:

1. Cut half of the head by slicing it lengthwise again.

2. In a small bowl, combine the chili garlic paste, sesame oil, soy sauce, salt, and stevia; place by the burner.

3. Heat the canola or peanut oil in a wok or greater pan over the highest heat. Start cooking the cabbage after adding it. Add the spice combination after about a minute; you want the cabbage to be mostly crunchy but just beginning to wilt. Rice vinegar should then be added, stirred one more, and served.

Nutritional Info: 115 cal, 8g fat (1g sag. fat), 3mg chol, 304mg sod, 8g carb (4g sugars, 2g fiber), 3g pro.

Asparagus with Sesame and Soy Mayonnaise

(Preparation Time: 5 minutes | Cooking Time: 5 minutes | Serving 2 | Difficulty: Easy)

Ingredients:

- ½ cup mayonnaise
- 1 teaspoon sesame oil, dark
- 1 scallion
- 1 pound asparagus
- 2 teaspoons soy sauce
- ¼ teaspoon chili garlic sauce

Instructions:

1. Asparagus should be cut where they naturally desire to break. Please put them in a glass pie dish or a steamer for the microwave. Add a few tablespoons of water, secure the lid, and microwave on high for five minutes.

2. While waiting, insert the other ingredients in your food processor, attach the S-blade, and process until the scallion is finely chopped.

3. Everyone receives a little pool of sauce to dip their asparagus in when this is served. For a more elegant presentation, put the sauce into a baggie, cut a little piece off the top and decorative pipe squiggles of sauce across your plates of asparagus.

4. It makes a great salad if you microwave the asparagus early in the morning and chill it.

Nutritional Info: 38 cal, 2g fat (0.4g sag. fat), 0mg chol, 1mg sod, 3g carb (0g sugars, 1g fiber), 1.9g pro.

Pepperoncini Spinach

(Preparation Time: 5 minutes | Cooking Time: 5 minutes | Serving 2 | Difficulty: Easy)

Ingredients:

- 1 ½ teaspoons olive oil
- 1 clove garlic
- 280 g 1 package frozen spinach, chopped and thawed
- 2 pepperoncini peppers, minced and drained
- 1 tablespoon lemon juice

Instructions:

1. You want to squeeze out all the extra water, so place the thawed spinach inside a strainer and compress it using the back of the spoon or your clean hands.

2. Spray some nonstick cooking spray in a medium skillet, then add the olive oil and heat it over medium-high heat. Add the spinach, garlic, and pepperoncini once it is heated. Sauté for approximately 5 minutes, stirring often. Add the lemon juice, simmer for one more minute, and then serve.

Nutritional Info: 30 cal, 1g fat (0g sag. fat), 0mg chol, 1mg sod, 5g carb (2g sugars, 3g fiber), 1g pro.

Roasted Asparagus

(Preparation Time: 5 minutes | Baking Time: 15 minutes | Serving 2 | Difficulty: Easy)

Ingredients:

- 1 tablespoon olive oil
- 3 pounds of asparagus, equal
- Ground black pepper and salt, to taste

Instructions:

1. The oven should be preheated to 450°F.

2. Each asparagus stalk should be gently bent until it snaps or breaks. Throw away the portion that was under the break.

3. Pour the olive oil into a shallow baking pan or ovenproof dish big enough to hold the asparagus. Add pepper and salt, preferably freshly ground.

4. Asparagus should be coated well with oil and spices before being placed in olive oil.

5. Place inside your preheated oven and bake for 5 to 7 minutes for thin spears, Eight to Ten at medium, and 12 to 15 minutes for thick spears, or until just tender.

6. Take out and serve right away.

7. The asparagus is excellent, but you can top it with your favorite sauces or brown butter and drizzle it on top. For more or less asparagus, change the spice and oil proportions.

Nutritional Info: 50 cal, 3g fat (1g sag. fat), 0mg chol, 50mg sod, 4g carb (1g sugars, 2g fiber), 3g pro.

Sesame Sautéed Spinach

(Preparation Time: 5 minutes | Cooking Time: 10 minutes | Serving 2 | Difficulty: Easy)

Ingredients:

- 1 tablespoon peanut or coconut oil
- 2 tablespoons soy sauce
- 1 tablespoon sesame seeds
- 1 pound fresh spinach

Instructions:

1. Over medium-high heat, place the sesame seeds inside a small, heavy pan and swirl or shake them until they are toasted and golden brown. Turn off the heat and set aside.

2. Use a wok if you have one for this recipe. If not, apply nonstick cooking spray on your big, heavy skillet. In either case, heat the oil in the pan at high heat. Add the spinach to the heated oil and stir-fry it until it wilts.

3. Add the soy sauce, then divide it among serving trays.

4. Serve each dish with ¾ teaspoon of toasted sesame seeds.

Nutritional Info: 102 cal, 7g fat (1g sag. fat), 0mg chol, 194mg sod, 7g carb (0g sugars, 4g fiber), 5g pro.

Herb Lemon Zucchini

(Preparation Time: 5 minutes | Cooking Time: 5 minutes | Serving 2 | Difficulty: Easy)

Ingredients:

- 2 tablespoons olive oil
- ½ teaspoon coriander, ground
- 1 minced clove garlic
- 2 zucchini, medium
- 2 tablespoons lemon juice
- ¼ teaspoon thyme, dried
- 2 tablespoons fresh parsley, chopped

Instructions:

1. Slice your zucchinis 1/4 inch thick after cutting them in half lengthwise.

2. Put your big, heavy skillet over medium-high heat after spraying it with nonstick cooking spray. Olive oil is added. When it's heated, add your thinly sliced zucchini and cook it while continuously turning it until it softens.

3. Add the garlic, thyme, coriander, and lemon juice. Stir everything together, lower the heat to medium, and simmer for a few more minutes.

4. Just before serving, add the parsley.

Nutritional Info: 410 cal, 13g fat (4g sag. fat), 140mg chol, 410mg sod, 13g carb (2g sugars, 3g fiber), 58g pro.

Mushrooms Sautéed and Pepperoni with Spinach

(Preparation Time: 5 minutes | Cooking Time: 5 minutes | Serving 2 | Difficulty: Easy)

Ingredients:

- 2 tablespoons divided olive oil
- 1 bunch of sliced scallions
- 140 g 1 bag baby spinach
- 1-ounce pepperoni, sliced
- 1 pound of mushrooms, sliced
- 2 crushed cloves of garlic
- Ground black pepper and salt, for taste

Instructions:

1. Cut the pepperoni into very thin pieces. In a big, heavy skillet, warm 1 tablespoon of olive oil. Add your pepperoni, and cook until crisp. Use a slotted spoon to lift out, and then drain on towels.

2. Heat the skillet with the last tablespoon of oil on a medium-high flame. Add the mushrooms and cook them for a few minutes or until they soften and brown. Sauté the thinly sliced scallions for a few more minutes or until they turn brown. Add the spinach after incorporating the garlic. Only after the spinach wilts, repeatedly turn the whole dish. Add the pepperoni

chunks after seasoning with pepper and salt to taste.

Nutritional Info: 107 cal, 9g fat (5g sag. fat), 22mg chol, 120mg sod, 5g carb (1g sugars, 2g fiber), 3g pro.

Cauliflower Garlic Stir-Fry

(Preparation Time: 5 minutes | Cooking Time: 5 minutes | Serving 2 | Difficulty: Easy)

Ingredients:

- 1 head cauliflower, large
- 1 tbsp. fresh parsley, minced
- 3 tbsp. margarine or butter
- 2 minced garlic cloves
- 1 ½ tsp. Pepper lemon seasoning

Instructions:

1. Melt butter in a pan over medium heat. Add garlic and cauliflower. Add some lemon pepper and parsley.

2. Stir and cook for twelve to fifteen minutes or until the food is soft and gently browned.

Nutritional Info: 63 cal, 4g fat (3g sag. fat), 0mg chol, 78mg sod, 5g carb (4g sugars, 2g fiber), 2g pro.

Chapter 4: Meat Recipes

Below are meat recipes, including chicken, turkey, beef, lamb and pork.

Chicken Burgers with Sun-Dried Tomatoes and Basil

(Preparation Time: 5 minutes | Cooking Time: 12 minutes | Serving 2 | Difficulty: Moderate)

Ingredients:

- 2 tablespoons sun-dried tomatoes, finely chopped
- 1 minced clove garlic
- 1 teaspoon fresh oregano, minced
- ½ teaspoon salt
- ¼ teaspoon cayenne
- 1 pound chicken, ground
- 2 tablespoons onion, minced
- 1 tablespoon fresh basil, minced
- 1 teaspoon paprika
- ¼ teaspoon ground black pepper

Instructions:

1. Add everything into a mixing basin and thoroughly stir it with clean hands. Shape into three patties. Put it on a dish and refrigerate them if you have some time.

2. For around five to six minutes on each side within the large, heavy skillet. Consider drizzling them with mayonnaise flavored with lemon juice and minced basil.

Nutritional Info: 210 cal, 3g fat (4g sag. fat), 95mg chol, 560mg sod, 3g carb (1g sugars, 1g fiber), 31g pro.

Roasted Tasty Chicken

(Preparation Time: 5 minutes | Cooking Time: 15 minutes | Serving 2 | Difficulty: Easy)

Ingredients:

- 1 heaping tablespoon of mayonnaise
- Paprika
- 5 pounds 1 whole chicken

- Ground black pepper and salt
- Onion powder

Instructions:

1. When the chicken is freezing, ensure it has fully thawed; if the center is still chilly, run more hot water into it until the middle is no longer frosty.

2. Remove the giblets from the body cavity if you've never cooked up an entire chicken. Put your chicken on a dish after drying it with paper towels. Be cautious not to taint the jar as you scoop the mayonnaise into a small plate. Give the chicken a good mayo massage with clean hands. That's correct; slather every square inch of the chicken's skin with mayonnaise. Thoroughly season the chicken with salt, paprika, pepper, and onion powder on both sides. Place the chicken on the rack in a deep roasting pan and cook in the oven.

Nutritional Info: 187 cal, 11g fat (3.1g sag. fat), 80mg chol, 60mg sod, 0g carb (0g sugars, 0g fiber), 20g pro.

Tandoori Chicken

(Preparation Time: 5 minutes | Cooking Time: 60 minutes | Serving 2 | Difficulty: Easy)

Ingredients:

- 1 ½ cups plain yogurt
- 2 tablespoons fresh ginger root, grated
- 2 teaspoons chili powder
- 1 teaspoon salt
- ½ teaspoon cumin, ground
- ½ teaspoon cloves, ground
- 2 whole bay leaves
- 5 pounds chicken thighs without skin, bone-in
- ¼ cup olive oil
- 1 tablespoon lemon juice
- 2 teaspoons turmeric, ground
- 1 teaspoon coriander, ground
- ½ teaspoon cinnamon, ground
- 4 cloves garlic

Instructions:

1. Blend the remaining ingredients in your blender until they form a sauce.

2. Flip each piece of chicken with tongs to cover with sauce after pouring it over the chicken.

3. The baking pan should be covered with plastic wrap, placed in the refrigerator, and set for at least 4 hours, ideally, a day.

4. Take the chicken out of your refrigerator and let it warm up.

5. While you wait, heat the oven to 350 degrees.

6. Pull the baking pan's plastic wrap off once the oven is heated and place it inside to cook. Using tongs to flip the chicken every 45 to 60 minutes while roasting.

Nutritional Info: 263 cal, 12g fat (4.2g sag. fat), 135mg chol, 132mg sod, 6.1g carb (3.7g sugars, 0.7g fiber), 31g pro.

Chicken Diavolo Skewers

(Preparation Time: 5 minutes | Cooking Time: 15 minutes | Serving 2 | Difficulty: Easy)

Ingredients:

- ¼ cup olive oil
- 2 minced cloves garlic
- Ground black pepper and salt, for taste
- 1 lemon, 6 wedges cut
- 2 pounds chicken thighs, skinless and boneless
- ¼ cup lemon juice
- 2 tablespoons red pepper flakes
- Fresh parsley to garnish

Instructions:

1. Bamboo skewers should be soaked in water for 30 minutes before cooking if you want to use them.

2. When it's ready to cook, please turn on the grill or the broiler, pour the marinade onto a dish, and set it aside. The chicken bits are threaded onto six skewers.

3. Now that they are cooked through, you may grill or broil them for approximately 8

minutes, frequently basting them with the marinade you set up. However, cease basting that has at least a few minutes left in the cooking process to ensure that all the bacteria from the raw chicken are destroyed.

4. If using, add some chopped parsley to each skewer's garnish and serve over a lemon slice for squeezing over the food.

Nutritional Info: 526 cal, 4g fat (1g sag. fat), 132mg chol, 960mg sod, 55g carb (9g sugars, 5g fiber), 62g pro.

Yucatán Chicken

(Preparation Time: 5 minutes | Cooking Time: 25 minutes | Serving 2 | Difficulty: Easy)

Ingredients:

- 1 tablespoon ground allspice, ground
- ½ teaspoon cumin, ground
- 1 teaspoon lemon juice
- 2 pounds chicken thighs
- 1 tablespoon black pepper, ground
- 1 teaspoon oregano, dried
- 1 teaspoon lime juice
- 3 drops of orange extract

Instructions:

1. Everything save the chicken should be combined. Apply this mixture evenly beneath the skin and all over the chicken thighs. For many hours, refrigerate.

2. When it's time to cook, prepare your broiler, place the chicken on the rack with the skin side down, and then broil for approximately 15 minutes at a distance of about six inches from the fire. Offer it another 10 as you turn. Give it another turn and at least five more minutes. Then, with the skin side up, puncture the piece to the bone. It's finished when the juice runs clear. You need to wait a bit longer if it becomes pink.

3. You could also grill this on the BBQ grill if you'd like. If you want to bring something to the beach or a park to grill while there, put the chicken in a large resealable plastic bag early in the day. Then take the

chicken pack, place it in the cooler, and go.

4. With a sizable green salad, serve.

Nutritional Info: 160 cal, 6g fat (1.5g sag. fat), 100mg chol, 570mg sod, 3g carb (2g sugars, 0g fiber), 21g pro.

Chicken Golden Triangle Kabobs

(Preparation Time: 5 minutes | Cooking Time: 15 minutes | Serving 2 | Difficulty: Easy)

Ingredients:

- 2 tablespoons lemon juice
- 1 minced shallot
- 1 tablespoon fresh ginger root, grated
- 3 drops of stevia liquid
- 1 ½ pounds chicken thighs, skinless and boneless
- 1 tablespoon lime juice
- 5 crushed cloves of garlic
- 2 tablespoons soy sauce
- 1 teaspoon turmeric, ground

Instructions:

1. Place the chicken cubes in a sealable plastic bag, combine the remaining ingredients and pour them over the top. As you close the bag, squeeze out any remaining air. Place the bag inside the refrigerator for a minimum of several hours. Put the bamboo skewers in water to soak if you plan to use them immediately.

2. When it's time for supper, turn on your grill or broiler.

3. Remove the bag from the refrigerator, pour the marinade into a small dish, and set the marinade aside. Put four skewers with the chicken cubes on them.

4. Start grilling or broiling your skewers after around 5 minutes. Your kabobs will be finished when you flip them over after 5 minutes and baste both sides with the marinade you set up.

Nutritional Info: 220 cal, 2.2g fat (0.5g sag. fat), 37mg chol, 760mg sod, 35g carb (27g sugars, 2.3g fiber), 15g pro.

Noodles and Creamy Chicken in a Bowl

(Preparation Time: 5 minutes | Cooking Time: 5 minutes | Serving 2 | Difficulty: Easy)

Ingredients:

- ¼ cup jarred red peppers, roasted
- 1 scallion
- 3 tablespoons onion and chive cream cheese
- Ground black pepper and salt, for taste
- 225 g 1 package fettuccini width tofu shirataki
- 5 Kalamata olives
- 1 tablespoon fresh parsley, minced
- 3 ounces chicken breast strips with Southwestern seasoning, precooked

Instructions:

1. Open the package of shirataki, drain, and rinse them before placing them in a dish that can be microwaved. 2 minutes on high in a microwave.

2. Drain, and then dice the roasted red peppers while that's going on.

3. Drain the shirataki one more when the microwave beeps. Reintroduce them for two more minutes.

4. Press the Kalamata with your thumb to release the pits, and then slice them up. Scallion should be cut into pieces, including the crisp green portion, and parsley should also be chopped.

5. Last but not least, drain your noodles. Add your cream cheese, and the chicken breast strips at this point, and microwave the mixture for 30 seconds.

6. Add the peppers, scallions, olives, and parsley after it has finished cooking. Add pepper and salt, stir until the cheese is melted, and then eat!

Nutritional Info: 274 cal, 8g fat (4g sag. fat), 76mg chol, 418mg sod, 25g carb (6g sugars, 3g fiber), 25g pro.

Oven-Fried Chicken Chops

(Preparation Time: 5 minutes | Cooking Time: 15 minutes | Serving 2 | Difficulty: Easy)

Ingredients:

- 1 tbsp. Paprika
- ¼ tsp. pepper
- 1 ½ cups dry milk, non-fat
- 2 tsp. poultry seasoning
- 4 chicken breast halves, skinless and boneless

Instructions:

1. Place the ingredients inside a large plastic bag that can be sealed. One piece of chicken or pig at a time is added and tossed to coat. Put the items in a nonstick cooking spray-coated 8-inch square baking pan.

2. Bake for 15 minutes at 350°F, uncovered, or until juices flow clear.

Nutritional Info: 240 cal, 4g fat (3g sag. fat), 78mg chol, 204mg sod, 15g carb (6g sugars, 3g fiber), 36g pro.

Garlic Cheese and Artichokes Stuffed Chicken Breasts

(Preparation Time: 5 minutes | Baking Time: 15 minutes | Serving 2 | Difficulty: Easy)

Ingredients:

- 170 g artichoke hearts, marinated drained
- ¼ teaspoon black pepper, ground
- 1 ½ pounds 4 chicken breast, skinless and boneless
- 3 ounces of garlic cheese
- ½ tablespoon butter

Instructions:

1. Place every chicken breast inside a large, heavy plastic bag that can be sealed,

one at a time, squeezing the air out as you go. The chicken should be pounded until it is ¼ inch over using any heavy, blunt object. Replicate with the remaining chicken breasts.

2. Put your cheese and artichoke hearts in a food processor with an engaged S-blade. Also include the pepper. Pulse the artichokes until they are finely chopped but not puréed.

3. Each breast should have a quarter of the cheese mixture spread before being rolled up like jelly. Use toothpicks to secure the closure.

4. Spray nonstick cooking spray in a big, heavy skillet and heat it to medium-high. When it is heated, add the butter and swirl it to coat the skillet's bottom. Add the chicken rolls now, and cook for 3 minutes on each side until they brown.

5. If the handle of your skillet is not oven-safe, cover it with foil. Place everything in the oven and bake for fifteen minutes until everything is cooked. Then, serve.

Nutritional Info: 210 cal, 8g fat (4g sag. fat), 85mg chol, 490mg sod, 7g carb (1g sugars, 1g fiber), 28g pro.

Herb-Lemon Chicken Breast

(Preparation Time: 5 minutes | Cooking Time: 15 minutes | Serving 2 | Difficulty: Easy)

Ingredients:

- ½ cup olive oil
- Ground black pepper and salt, to taste
- 2 tablespoons water
- 2 tablespoons fresh parsley, minced
- 2 crushed cloves of garlic
- 1 pound chicken breast, skinless and boneless
- 1 lemon
- ¼ cup fresh basil, minced

Instructions:

1. Spray some nonstick cooking spray on a skillet and place it over hot heat.

2. Grab a blunt, heavy instrument and your chicken, and then pound the chicken breast until it is an equal ½ inch thick. Cut each part into three pieces, and season both sides with salt and pepper.

3. Your now-hot pan should be filled with half of the garlicky olive oil. After swirling it around, add the chicken. Cover with an inclined lid that leaves a crack for three to four minutes.

4. Flip your chicken once the bottom has become golden. Give it another three to four minutes before re-covering with the tipped lid. Roll your lemon beneath your hand while firmly pushing down in the meantime. It will assist it in producing more juice. Slice your lemon in half, and then use the point of a knife to remove the seeds.

5. Squeeze one of your lemon halves over the chicken once all sides are browned. Turn the burner to medium-low, flip it over to coat all sides, and then cover it back up. Cook it completely if necessary.

6. After plating the chicken, add the water and the other half of the lemon juice to the pan. Pour it over the chicken after stirring it together with a fork to scrape off the nice brown pieces. Serve after adding the leftover garlic olive oil & herbs on top.

Nutritional Info: 350 cal, 6g fat (2g sag. fat), 50mg chol, 850mg sod, 51g carb (4g sugars, 4g fiber), 22g pro.

Creamy Horseradish Sauce Chicken

(Preparation Time: 5 minutes | Cooking Time: 15 minutes | Serving 2 | Difficulty: Easy)

Ingredients:

- 1 tablespoon butter

- ¾ cup chicken broth

- 1 tablespoon horseradish, prepared

- Optional: ¼ cup heavy cream xanthan or Guar

- 4 pounds chicken pieces, cut-up

- 1 tablespoon olive oil

- 1 ½ teaspoons chicken concentrate bouillon

- 4 ounces of cream cheese

- Ground black pepper and salt, for taste

Instructions:

1. The chicken should be browned in butter and olive oil over medium-high heat in your large, heavy pan. Add to the cooker.

2. Horseradish, chicken broth, and bouillon powder are all combined. Add to the chicken. Cook for 10 minutes with the lid on and the cooker on high.

3. Pull out your chicken and place it on a tray when the timer goes off. Cream cheese should be cut into bits and melted into the sauce before heavy cream is added.

4. Xanthan or guar shakers may be used to thicken if you feel it requires it. Add pepper and salt to your liking before serving.

Nutritional Info: 166.8 cal, 5.3g fat (0.8g sag. fat), 58mg chol, 440mg sod, 1.5g carb (0.3g sugars, 0.1g fiber), 23.1g pro.

Creamy Orange Sauce Chicken

(Preparation Time: 5 minutes | Cooking Time: 15 minutes | Serving 2 | Difficulty: Easy)

Ingredients:

- 3 tablespoons oil

- ½ cup lemon juice

- 1 teaspoon orange zest, grated

- ¼ teaspoon liquid stevia

- 6 ounces of cream cheese

- 4 pounds chicken thighs, skinless

- ½ cup white wine vinegar
- 3 tablespoons brandy
- ½ teaspoon orange extract
- 8 sliced scallions
- Ground black pepper and salt, for taste

Instructions:

1. Over moderate flame, brown the chicken all over in the oil in a large, heavy skillet, to the cooker, transfer.

2. Orange zest, brandy, orange extract, stevia, and white wine vinegar combine. Add to the chicken. Cook for approximately 12 minutes on high in a covered saucepan in a cooker.

3. Transfer your chicken to a dish when the cooking period is over. Sliced scallions should be added to the liquid inside the saucepan, after which pieces of cream cheese should be added and stirred until melted. Add salt and pepper to taste. Over the chicken, serve the sauce.

Nutritional Info: 679.3 cal, 14.4g fat (7.2g sag. fat), 235mg chol, 491mg sod, 35.5g carb (24.4g sugars, 2.7g fiber), 87.5g pro.

Italian Chicken

(Preparation Time: 5 minutes | Cooking Time: 8 minutes | Serving 2 | Difficulty: Easy)

Ingredients:

- 14 ½ oz. 1 tin Italian tomatoes, stewed
- ½ tsp. basil, dried
- 1 tbsp. cornstarch
- Hot spaghetti, cooked
- 4 chicken breast halves, skinless and boneless
- 4 oz. 1 tin mushroom pieces and stems, drained
- ¼ tsp. garlic powder
- 1/3 cup cold water

Instructions:

1. Cook the chicken for four to six minutes on each side, or until the juices run clear, in a large skillet sprayed with nonstick cooking spray.

2. Meanwhile, in a saucepan, cook tomatoes, basil, mushrooms, and garlic powder on medium heat.

3. To the tomato mixture, add the cornflour and water combination. Regain a boil and stir, and cook for a further two minutes. Chicken is served over spaghetti, with tomato sauce on top.

Nutritional Info: 177 cal, 3g fat (2g sag. fat), 73mg chol, 178mg sod, 7g carb (5g sugars, 2g fiber), 28g pro.

Turkey Super-Easy Divan

(Preparation Time: 5 minutes | Baking Time: 30 minutes | Serving 2 | Difficulty: Easy)

Ingredients:

- 1 pound turkey, sliced roasted
- 1 cup mayonnaise
- 2 tablespoons dry vermouth
- 1 pound broccoli, frozen and thawed
- 1 cup Parmesan, divided grated
- 1 cup heavy cream

Instructions:

1. Set the oven to 350°F. Spray nonstick cooking spray in an 8-inch square baking dish.

2. The broccoli should fill the pan's bottom.

3. Turkey's leftover slices should be spread over the broccoli. To give folks a choice, I prefer to place the dark meat on one side with the white flesh on the other.

4. All except 2 tablespoons of the Parmesan should be combined with the mayonnaise, vermouth, and cream in a mixing bowl. Pour over the broccoli and turkey.

5. Top with the remaining Parmesan cheese. Bake for approximately 30 minutes or until it begins to turn brown.

Nutritional Info: 354.6 cal, 12.7g fat (3.3g sag. fat), 61.5mg chol, 2084mg sod, 32.3g carb (6g sugars, 6.2g fiber), 29.8g pro.

Weekend Thanksgiving Curry

(Preparation Time: 5 minutes | Cooking Time: 15 minutes | Serving 2 | Difficulty: Easy)

Ingredients:

- 2 teaspoons garam masala
- 1 teaspoon turmeric, ground
- 2 crushed cloves of garlic
- 1 teaspoon cayenne
- ¾ cup turkey or chicken broth
- Salt, for taste
- 3 tablespoons coconut oil
- 1 teaspoon cinnamon, ground
- ½ onion, medium chopped
- 1 tablespoon ginger root, freshly grated
- 425 ml 1 tin coconut milk, unsweetened
- 560 g or 4 cups diced turkey, cooked

Instructions:

1. Melt coconut oil in a large, heavy skillet by setting it to medium-low heat. For about a minute, stir after adding the garam masala, turmeric, and cinnamon.
2. The onion should be added and sautéed until transparent.
3. Add the ginger, cayenne, and garlic at this time. Add the chicken broth and coconut milk. It would help if you stirred it until it became a creamy sauce.
4. Turn the flame to low and stir in the turkey. Allow the mixture to boil for about 15 minutes.
5. Serve in dishes with soup spoons and salt to taste.

Nutritional Info: 560 cal, 16g fat (14g sag. fat), 0mg chol, 680mg sod, 93g carb (9g sugars, 7g fiber), 12g pro.

Jakarta Steak

(Preparation Time: 5 minutes | Cooking Time: 12 minutes | Serving 2 | Difficulty: Easy)

Ingredients:

- 2 tablespoons soy sauce
- 2 teaspoons fresh ginger root, grated
- 1 teaspoon black pepper, ground
- 2 crushed cloves of garlic
- 2 pounds trimmed sirloin steak
- 1 tablespoon lime juice
- 1 teaspoon turmeric, ground
- 12 drops liquid stevia

Instructions:

1. You may broil this or cook it on your BBQ grill. Start your charcoal grill at least 30 minutes before you want to cook. In any case, cook it on the grill or under the broiler until it is cooked to your preference, turning it halfway through to baste both sides using the marinade.
2. Before cutting and serving, let your steak five minutes to rest. To eliminate any lingering bacteria, boil the leftover marinade vigorously for several minutes before spooning a little over each dish.

Nutritional Info: 614 cal, 41g fat (16g sag. fat), 214mg chol, 115mg sod, 0g carb (0g sugars, 0g fiber), 58g pro.

Wine Sauce Rib-Eye Steak

(Preparation Time: 5 minutes | Baking Time: 15 minutes | Serving 2 | Difficulty: Easy)

Ingredients:

- 1 tablespoon olive oil
- ½ cup red wine, dry
- 1 tablespoon balsamic vinegar
- 1 teaspoon Dijon or brown mustard
- Ground black pepper and salt, for taste
- 1 ½ pounds rib-eye steak
- 2 shallots
- ½ cup beef stock
- 1 tablespoon thyme, dried
- 3 tablespoons butter

Instructions:

1. Place all of the ingredients for the wine sauce in a measuring cup having a pouring lip, cut your shallots, and mix the

wine, vinegar, beef stock, mustard, and thyme. Together, whisk them.

2. Flip the steak over and start the timer once the alarm goes off.

3. When the steak is finished cooking, lay it on a dish and keep it somewhere warm. Pour your wine mixture into a skillet, scraping off any tasty brown bits as you go, and then start a vigorous boil. Your sauce should continue to simmer until it has reduced by at least half. Serve the butter with your steak after melting it and adding pepper and salt.

Nutritional Info: 187 cal, 11.4g fat (1.4g sag. fat), 0mg chol, 88mg sod, 1.7g carb (0.9g sugars, 0.1g fiber), 19.5g pro.

Smothered Burgers

(Preparation Time: 5 minutes | Cooking Time: 5 minutes | Serving 2 | Difficulty: Easy)

Ingredients:

- 2 tablespoons butter or olive oil
- ½ cup mushrooms, sliced
- 1 dash of soy sauce
- 1 ½ pounds ground chuck in 2 patties
- ½ cup onion, sliced
- 1/8 teaspoon anchovy paste

Instructions:

1. Begin preparing your burgers according to your favorite way. Melt the butter over medium heat inside a small, sturdy skillet while that's going on.

2. Sauté the mushrooms and onion together before the onion is transparent. Soy sauce and anchovy paste should be combined. Over the burgers, spoon the onion-mushroom mixture.

Nutritional Info: 511 cal, 28.6g fat (12g sag. fat), 98mg chol, 1071mg sod, 20.6g carb (4.5g sugars, 4g fiber), 29g pro.

Broiled Pan Steak

(Preparation Time: 5 minutes | Cooking Time: 12 minutes | Serving 2 | Difficulty: Easy)

Ingredients:

- 1 tablespoon bacon grease or olive oil
- 1 ½ pounds steak, 1 inch thick (any rib eye, sirloin, T-bone, or strip)

Instructions:

1. Add the oil or bacon grease to the heated pan, stir it around, but then add the steak. Set a timer for about 5 or 6 minutes; the exact duration will vary on your intended degree of doneness and how high your burner gets. A 1-inch-thick steak cooks to medium rare for 5 minutes on each side.

2. Flip the steak over and start the timer once the alarm goes off. After the allotted time has passed, let the steak sit on a dish for five minutes before eating.

Nutritional Info: 470 cal, 18g fat (4g sag. fat), 70mg chol, 570mg sod, 40g carb (7g sugars, 5g fiber), 36g pro.

Meatza

(Preparation Time: 5 minutes | Baking Time: 25 minutes | Serving 2 | Difficulty: Easy)

Ingredients:

- ¾ pound Italian sausage
- 2 teaspoons dried oregano or Italian seasoning
- 1 cup pizza sauce without sugar
- 8 ounces of mozzarella cheese, shredded
- ¾ pound beef, ground
- 1/3 cup onion, minced
- 1 crushed clove garlic
- Optional: 3 tablespoons Romano or Parmesan cheese, grated

Instructions:

1. With clean hands, mix the meat and sausage with the onion, garlic, Italian seasoning, and oil in a large bowl. Mix thoroughly. In a baking pan, pat this out into a uniform layer. For 20 minutes, bake.

2. Due to the fat cooking off, the meat will significantly decrease in size after it has finished cooking. Pour the grease out. Over the meat, smear the pizza sauce.

3. If desired, top the sauce with a sprinkle of Parmesan before sprinkling the top with the shredded mozzarella. Your broiler should be on a high.

4. You Meatza put it! About 5 minutes of broiling should be plenty to melt and start browning the cheese.

Nutritional Info: 360 cal, 20.4g fat (6.6g sag. fat), 34mg chol, 652mg sod, 27g carb (1.7g sugars, 1.3g fiber), 17.7g pro.

Lime-Anaheim Marinade Sirloin

(Preparation Time: 5 minutes | Cooking Time: 45 minutes | Serving 2 | Difficulty: Moderate)

Ingredients:

- 1/3 cup lime juice
- ¼ teaspoon black pepper, ground
- 2 cloves garlic
- 1 ½ pounds trimmed sirloin steak
- 2 tablespoons olive oil
- ½ Anaheim chile pepper

Instructions:

1. Place the S-blade on your food processor, add the other ingredients, and pulse until the garlic and pepper are completely pureed. Over the meat, pour the marinade. Give everything a minimum of 30 minutes to sit; ideally, an hour or more.

2. Prepare the grill or broiler. With the marinade still on hand, remove your steak from it. Grill or broil your steak at a heat that is not quite high enough to burn it. When flipping the steak, baste all sides with the marinade, and discard it since you want the heat to destroy any bacteria before the steak is finished.

3. Before cutting and serving, let the steak for five minutes to rest.

Nutritional Info: 340 cal, 13g fat (2.5g sag. fat), 34mg chol, 640mg sod, 42g carb (4g sugars, 7.1g fiber), 17g pro.

Florentine Burger Scramble

(Preparation Time: 5 minutes | Baking Time: 20 minutes | Serving 2 | Difficulty: Easy)

Ingredients:

- ½ cup onion, finely diced
- 8 ounces softened cream cheese
- ½ cup Parmesan cheese, shredded
- 1 ½ pounds lean ground beef
- 280 g 1 package chopped frozen spinach, drained and thawed
- ½ cup heavy cream
- Ground black pepper and salt, for taste

Instructions:

1. The onion and ground beef should be browned in a sizable ovenproof pan.

2. When the meat is finished, add your spinach and continue to simmer. Pepper and salt to taste, the heavy cream and Parmesan. Uniformly distribute in the skillet after thoroughly mixing.

3. Bake for about 20 minutes, uncovered, or until bubbling and browned over the top.

Nutritional Info: 625 cal, 52g fat (25g sag. fat), 175mg chol, 439mg sod, 3.1g carb (0.2g sugars, 1g fiber), 35g pro.

Bleu Burger

(Preparation Time: 5 minutes | Cooking Time: 5 minutes | Serving 2 | Difficulty: Easy)

Ingredients:

- 2 tablespoons blue cheese, crumbled
- 12 ounces chuck, ground in the patties
- 2 teaspoons sweet red onion, finely minced

Instructions:

1. Use whichever manner you like to cook the burger. Add the blue cheese and let it melt when it's nearly done to your taste. Place on a platter after being taken off the heat, then top over the onion.

Nutritional Info: 623 cal, 32g fat (13g sag. fat), 144mg chol, 969mg sod, 30g carb (4.5g sugars, 1.2g fiber), 49g pro.

Joe

(Preparation Time: 5 minutes | Cooking Time: 7 minutes | Serving 2 | Difficulty: Easy)

Ingredients:

- 280 g 1 package frozen spinach, chopped and thawed
- 2 cloves garlic
- Ground black pepper and salt, for taste
- 1 ½ pounds of ground beef
- 1 onion, medium
- 6 eggs
- 1/3 cup Parmesan cheese, shredded

Instructions:

1. Add the garlic and onion once your ground beef is halfway done, and continue cooking until the meat is fully cooked. If you'd like, pour the excess fat off. Now combine the meat with the spinach. Allow the mixture to cook for about 5 minutes.

2. With a fork, thoroughly combine the eggs and then toss them into the meat mixture.

3. Once the eggs are set, mix and simmer for a further couple of minutes over moderate heat. Serve with the Parmesan cheese on top after seasoning with salt & pepper to taste.

Nutritional Info: 215 cal, 9.5g fat (4.4g sag. fat), 111mg chol, 704mg sod, 19g carb (12g sugars, 0.1g fiber), 30g pro.

Zucchini Italiano Meat Loaf

(Preparation Time: 5 minutes | Baking Time: 90 minutes | Serving 2 | Difficulty: Easy)

Ingredients:

- 1 chopped onion, medium
- Few tablespoons of Olive oil
- ¾ cup Parmesan cheese, grated
- 2 tablespoons fresh parsley, snipped
- ½ teaspoon black pepper, ground
- 2 chopped zucchini, medium
- 2 crushed cloves of garlic

- 1 ½ pounds chuck ground
- 3 tablespoons olive oil
- 1 teaspoon salt
- 1 egg

Instructions:

1. For around 7 to 8 minutes, sauté the onion, zucchini, and garlic inside the olive oil.

2. After cooling it, please place it in a large bowl with the other ingredients.

3. Mix well with clean hands. It will result in a fairly soft dough that you can shape on the broiler rack or place in a large loaf pan if you prefer.

4. When the juices flow clear, but it hasn't dried up, bake for between 75 and 90 minutes.

Nutritional Info: 204 cal, 10g fat (3.9g sag. fat), 108mg chol, 0mg sod, 7.7g carb (3.7g sugars, 0.7g fiber), 19.7g pro.

Beef Pepperoncini

(Preparation Time: 5 minutes | Cooking Time: 15 minutes | Serving 2 | Difficulty: Easy)

Ingredients:

- 1 cup pepperoncini peppers, including vinegar
- Xanthan or guar
- 2 pounds chuck pot roast, boneless
- ½ onion, medium chopped
- Ground black pepper and salt, for taste

Instructions:

1. Place the onion on top of the pepperoncini and pepperoncini on top of the meat in the cooker. Place the cover on, turn the burner high, and wait 15 minutes.

2. When done, remove the peppers with a slotted spoon, lay them on top of the roast, and then transfer the cooked meat to a dish. Serve the roast with the pot juices slightly thickened with the xanthan, guar, pepper, and salt to taste.

Nutritional Info: 275 cal, 20g fat (8.3g sag. fat), 80mg chol, 865mg sod, 1.6g carb (0g sugars, 0.3g fiber), 19g pro.

Roman Stew

(Preparation Time: 5 minutes | Cooking Time: 10 minutes | Serving 2 | Difficulty: Easy)

Ingredients:

- 1 onion, large chopped
- 1 ½ cups beef broth
- 1 teaspoon beef bouillon concentrates
- 8 ounces of cream cheese
- 1 pound beef round, chopped 1-inch cubes
- 2 tins mushrooms, sliced
- 2 teaspoons Worcestershire sauce
- 1 teaspoon paprika
- 8 ounces of sour cream

Instructions:

1. Work in a few batches to evenly brown the meat in the oil in your large, heavy pan over medium-high heat.
2. Place in a cooker.
3. After adding the garlic and celery, season everything with the other ingredients. Pour the wine and the canned tomatoes over everything at this point. Cook for seven to eight minutes with the lid on and the heat on high. The pot fluids may be somewhat thickened, although it's not required.

Nutritional Info: 353 cal, 39g fat (4g sag. fat), 158mg chol, 964mg sod, 5.5g carb (2.7g sugars, 1.6g fiber), 48g pro.

Italian Easy Beef

(Preparation Time: 5 minutes | Cooking Time: 5 minutes | Serving 2 | Difficulty: Easy)

Ingredients:

- 2 tablespoons olive oil
- 1 tablespoon beef bouillon concentrates
- ½ teaspoon oregano, dried
- ¼ teaspoon onion powder

- Ground black pepper and salt, for taste
- 2 pounds beef chuck
- ½ cup beef broth
- ¾ teaspoon lemon pepper
- ½ teaspoon garlic powder
- 12 drops liquid stevia

Instructions:

1. Scrap the good brown stuff so it melts and combine it with everything else in the pan, save the last pinch of salt and pepper. Place the cooker high, cover the pan, and pour this mixture over the steak. For six to eight minutes, cook.
2. Season to taste with pepper and salt after the cooking time is complete.

Nutritional Info: 384 cal, 15g fat (6g sag. fat), 127mg chol, 1639mg sod, 12g carb (2g sugars, 2g fiber), 45g pro.

Camembert Sauce Pork

(Preparation Time: 5 minutes | Cooking Time: 10 minutes | Serving 2 | Difficulty: Easy)

Ingredients:

- 2 ounces of Camembert cheese
- 3 tablespoons dry white wine
- 1/3 cup sour cream
- Ground black pepper, for taste
- 1 pound pork loin, boneless
- 1 tablespoon butter
- 1 tablespoon fresh sage, chopped
- 1 ½ teaspoons Dijon mustard

Instructions:

1. Spray nonstick cooking spray in a big, heavy skillet and heat it to medium-high. Include the butter. After the butter has melted or the pan is very hot, add the pork and swirl the butter about the bottom of the pan.
2. Cook the boneless pork loin until it turns gently brown on both sides. Place the platter with the meat in a warm location.
3. Swirl the wine into the pan with a spatula while collecting all the savory brown

pieces. Sage has been added; stir once more. Reduce the temperature to medium-low. Put the Camembert bits in now. Once the cheese has fully melted, toss them around and break up the larger lumps with your spatula. After adding the pepper to taste and whisking in the mustard and sour cream, the dish is finished.

Nutritional Info: 417 cal, 22.3g fat (10g sag. fat), 165mg chol, 238mg sod, 3g carb (2.6g sugars, 1.1g fiber), 44g pro.

Orange Topped Chops

(Preparation Time: 5 minutes | Cooking Time: 15 minutes | Serving 2 | Difficulty: Easy)

Ingredients:

- 1 tbsp. vegetable oil
- ½ tsp. cloves, ground
- 6 pork chops
- 11 oz. 1 tin mandarin oranges, drained
- Pepper, for taste

Instructions:

1. Pork chops should be browned in oil on all sides in a pan. Oranges are placed on top, and then pepper and cloves are added.

2. 15 minutes, with the lid on, or until the beef juices are clear.

Nutritional Info: 167 cal, 7g fat (3g sag. fat), 52mg chol, 39mg sod, 6g carb (4g sugars, 1g fiber), 11g pro.

Beef Stroganoff

(Preparation Time: 5 minutes | Cooking Time: 10 minutes | Serving 2 | Difficulty: Easy)

Ingredients:

- 3 tablespoons olive oil
- 4 cloves garlic
- ¼ teaspoon cinnamon, ground
- ¼ teaspoon black pepper, ground
- 1/8 teaspoon nutmeg, ground
- ½ cup dry red wine

- 3 pounds beef stew meat cubes
- 2 cups celery, sliced
- 1 teaspoon salt
- ¼ teaspoon cloves, ground
- 1/8 teaspoon allspice, ground
- 410 g 1 tin tomatoes, diced

Instructions:

1. In the cooker, place the meat. Place the mushroom juice and everything on top of the onion.

2. Pour the beef broth over everything after combining it with Worcestershire sauce, paprika, and bouillon powder.

3. For eight to ten minutes, cook.

4. Cut your cream cheese into chunks and toss them into the soup inside the cooker before it has melted just before serving. Serve after adding the sour cream.

Nutritional Info: 391 cal, 23g fat (11g sag. fat), 115mg chol, 300mg sod, 21g carb (3g sugars, 1g fiber), 25g pro.

Kalua Pig and Cabbage

(Preparation Time: 5 minutes | Cooking Time: 1 hour | Serving 2 | Difficulty: Easy)

Ingredients:

- 2 teaspoons sea salt
- 1 head cabbage
- 1 pound Boston butt pork roast
- 1 tablespoon liquid smoke flavoring
- ¼ onion, medium

Instructions:

1. Salt the roast generously, covering every square inch of the top, and lightly massage it. Apply the smoke flavoring in the same manner.

2. The day before you want to serve, mince your onion and cut your cabbage pretty finely.

3. Pull out your pork; it will crumble and smell amazing. With a fork, shred it and place it in a large basin. If the meat requires more moisture, scoop off some of the liquid from

the saucepan. Then keep it in a warm location.

4. The leftover liquid should be poured over the cabbage and onion and mixed.

5. You want it to be wilted but still somewhat crunchy, so cover the pot, turn the cooker high, and let it simmer for at least an hour.

6. Together, serve both meat and cabbage.

Nutritional Info: 480 cal, 30g fat (13g sag. fat), 5mg chol, 1030mg sod, 4g carb (1.6g sugars, 1.1g fiber), 50g pro.

Balsamic Onions and Mustard-Grilled Pork

(Preparation Time: 5 minutes | Cooking Time: 5 minutes | Serving 2 | Difficulty: Easy)

Ingredients:

- 1 ½ pounds pork shoulder steaks, boneless
- 1 ½ tablespoons olive oil
- 2 tablespoons divided brown mustard
- 1 large red onion, thinly sliced
- 1 tablespoon balsamic vinegar

Instructions:

1. Over medium-high heat, begin sautéing the onion inside the olive oil in a large, heavy skillet. It would help if your onion was soft and turned brown, not tender-crisp. Add the balsamic vinegar once it has browned well. Place aside.

2. Your pork is now cooked. On the pork, apply the last 2 tablespoons of the mustard. Serve the steaks with the

balsamic-onion mixture divided among them.

Nutritional Info: 126 cal, 4g fat (1g sag. fat), 49mg chol, 54mg sod, 4g carb (1.6g sugars, 1.2g fiber), 16g pro.

Maple-Bourbon Glazed Pork Chops

(Preparation Time: 5 minutes | Cooking Time: 9 minutes | Serving 2 | Difficulty: Easy)

Ingredients:

12 ounces pork loin chops

- 1 crushed clove garlic
- 1 ½ tablespoon erythritol
- 5 drops of maple extract
- 1 tablespoon olive oil
- ¼ cup onion, minced
- ¼ cup chicken broth
- 1 tablespoon bourbon

Instructions:

1. Reduce the heat to medium-low after removing the chops from the pan.

2. Add the garlic and onion and cook for a minute in the lingering grease. Add the maple extract, erythritol, bourbon, and broth. With your spatula, stir this mixture while scraping off all the delicious brown pieces that have adhered to the pan.

3. Replacing the chops in the skillet. Set a timer for three minutes and lower the heat. Flip the chops over and start the timer three minutes after it goes off. The liquid ought to have thickened and boiled down at this point.

4. Put your chops on plates for serving, then spoon the glaze with garlic and onion chunks.

Nutritional Info: 770 cal, 28g fat (7g sag. fat), 195mg chol, 210mg sod, 62g carb (42g sugars, 2g fiber), 66g pro.

Ginger Tokyo Pork Chops

(Preparation Time: 5 minutes | Cooking Time: 13 minutes | Serving 2 | Difficulty: Easy)

Ingredients:

- 2 tablespoons soy sauce
- 1 ½ teaspoons dry sherry
- 12 ounces pork chops
- 2 teaspoons fresh ginger root, grated
- 1 tablespoon coconut oil

Instructions:

1. Spray nonstick cooking spray in a big, heavy skillet and heat it to medium-high. Add your coconut oil after letting it get nice and hot. To coat the skillet's bottom, swirl it around. After letting the marinade run off, please pick up the chops and place them in the skillet. They need to be lightly browned for five minutes on each side.

2. To serve, scrape all your pan juices over the chops and pour the leftover marinade over them. Reduce the heat and let the chops simmer for five to eight minutes or before done.

Nutritional Info: 730 cal, 36g fat (13g sag. fat), 140mg chol, 760mg sod, 63g carb (13g sugars, 4g fiber), 39g pro.

Pork Loin with Walnuts and Red Wine

(Preparation Time: 5 minutes | Cooking Time: 5 minutes | Serving 2 | Difficulty: Easy)

Ingredients:

- 1 pound pork loin, boneless
- ½ cup dry red wine
- 1 minced clove garlic
- ¼ cup fresh parsley, chopped
- 2 tablespoons divided butter
- 1 small sliced onion
- ½ teaspoon beef bouillon concentrates
- ¼ cup walnuts, chopped

Instructions:

1. Let the remaining half of the butter melts in the skillet. The onion should be added and sautéed until limp. The pork should be placed on top of an equal layer of onion in the pan.

2. Combine the wine, garlic, and beef bouillon powder. Pour it onto the pork, cover your pan with a tilted lid, lower the heat, and simmer the mixture for 20 minutes.

3. While waiting, toast the walnuts in the leftover 1 1/2 tablespoons of butter inside a small pan over medium heat for 5 minutes or until they begin to smell toasted. Turn off the heat and set aside.

4. Add your parsley to the skillet when the timer goes off. Allow the mixture to boil for a further five min or so. Serve each portion with a tablespoon of walnuts and pan juices.

Nutritional Info: 394 cal, 8.2g fat (2.8g sag. fat), 148mg chol, 418mg sod, 6.7g carb (0.9g sugars, 0.2g fiber), 48.3g pro.

Maple-Mustard Glazed Pork Steak

(Preparation Time: 5 minutes | Cooking Time: 15 minutes | Serving 2 | Difficulty: Easy)

Ingredients:

- Ground black pepper and salt, for taste
- ¼ cup chicken
- 1 tablespoon Dijon or spicy brown mustard
- 2 pounds of pork shoulder steaks
- 1 tablespoon olive oil
- 1 tablespoon erythritol
- 5 drops of maple extract

Instructions:

1. Place everything else in a mixing bowl and near the burner.

2. Turn the pork steaks over after approximately 5 minutes and cook them on the opposite side with a slanted cover.

3. Put your pork steaks on a dish when they are nearly done. As you whisk the mustard-maple mixture and scrape out any nice brown pieces, pour the mixture into the pan. Let it boil vigorously until it has reduced by almost half. Re-add the

steaks, turn them over to coat, and heat everything for one more minute or until the sauce has the texture of half-and-half. The sauce should be poured over the steaks before serving.

Nutritional Info: 186 cal, 4.8g fat (1g sag. fat), 73mg chol, 472mg sod, 9.3g carb (6.1g sugars, 0.1g fiber), 23g pro.

Lamb Mediterranean Burgers

(Preparation Time: 5 minutes | Cooking Time: 10 minutes | Serving 2 | Difficulty: Easy)

Ingredients:

- 2 tablespoons sun-dried tomatoes, chopped
- 1 tablespoon pesto sauce
- ½ teaspoon salt
- 2 tablespoons pine nuts
- ¼ onion, medium
- 1 pound lamb, ground
- 1 tablespoon garlic, chopped
- ¼ teaspoon black pepper, ground
- 3 ounces chèvre

Instructions:

1. If the sun-dried tomatoes are all in halves instead of being already chopped, cut them up. Next, chop your onion. Cut them up a little more, even if they are already chopped. Please put all of them in a mixing basin.

2. Add the pesto, salt, garlic, and pepper to the ground lamb. Mix it all together with clean palms until it is well combined. Make

three patties out of the mixture, and then grill them. Set a five-minute timer.

3. Toast the pine nuts in a dry pan until they are golden while the burgers cook.

4. When your burgers are finished cooking, dish them, top them with one ounce of chèvre crumbles, and then top them with pine nuts.

Nutritional Info: 710 cal, 36g fat (14g sag. fat), 100mg chol, 1670mg sod, 56g carb (7g sugars, 3g fiber), 40g pro.

Country Style Maple-Spice Ribs

(Preparation Time: 5 minutes | Cooking Time: 20 minutes | Serving 2 | Difficulty: Easy)

Ingredients:

- 2/3 cup erythritol
- ¼ cup chicken broth
- ½ teaspoon cinnamon, ground
- ½ teaspoon allspice, ground
- 1/8 teaspoon cayenne
- 3 crushed cloves garlic
- 3 pounds pork ribs, country-style
- ¼ cup onion, chopped
- 2 tablespoons soy sauce
- ½ teaspoon ginger, ground
- ¼ teaspoon black pepper, ground
- 1/8 teaspoon maple extract

Instructions:

1. In your cooker, place the country-style ribs. Pour over the ribs after combining everything else.

2. Cook over high for twenty minutes with the lid on.

Nutritional Info: 188 cal, 9g fat (3g sag. fat), 72mg chol, 226mg sod, 2.3g carb (0.1g sugars, 0.3g fiber), 22g pro.

Feta, Lamb, and Spinach Burgers

(Preparation Time: 5 minutes | Cooking Time: 5 minutes | Serving 2 | Difficulty: Easy)

Ingredients:

- ¼ cup onion, minced
- 1 teaspoon basil, dried
- ¼ teaspoon black pepper, ground
- 1 clove garlic, finely minced
- ½ cup feta cheese, crumbled
- 12 Kalamata olives, chopped and pitted
- 280 g 1 package chopped frozen spinach, drained and thawed
- 1 tablespoon lemon juice
- ¼ teaspoon salt
- 1 egg
- 1 ¼ pounds ground lamb
- ¼ cup sun-dried tomatoes, chopped

Instructions:

1. Add the onion, basil, lemon juice, salt, egg, pepper, and garlic after transferring it to a large bowl.

2. Stir everything together well.

3. The lamb, tomatoes, feta, and olives may now be added. Mix everything with clean hands until it is well blended. Create 6 patties that are at least 1 inch thick.

4. Warm up your tabletop electric grill. Based on how well-cooked you want your burgers to be, throw them on the grill for 6 to 8 minutes.

Nutritional Info: 623 cal, 35g fat (14g sag. fat), 147mg chol, 768mg sod, 42g carb (10g sugars, 3g fiber), 34g pro.

Chipotle-Maple Glazed Pork Steaks

(Preparation Time: 5 minutes | Cooking Time: 10 minutes | Serving 2 | Difficulty: Easy)

Ingredients:

- 1 tablespoon coconut oil or bacon grease
- 2 teaspoons brown mustard, spicy
- 2 crushed cloves of garlic
- 2 pounds of pork shoulder steaks
- ¼ cup erythritol

- 3 chipotle chiles tinned inside adobo sauce
- 6 drops of maple extract

Instructions:

1. Blend or process the other ingredients until the garlic and chipotle are finely chopped.

2. Once both sides of the steaks are browned, add your glaze to the pan and turn the steaks over to cover all sides. The steaks should be fully cooked, and the glaze should have somewhat reduced, which should take around 10 minutes. Serve the steaks while spooning the entire glaze from the pan over them.

Nutritional Info: 640 cal, 28g fat (9g sag. fat), 115mg chol, 240mg sod, 57g carb (25g sugars, 9g fiber), 42g pro.

Lamb Steaks with Olives, Lemon, and Capers

(Preparation Time: 5 minutes | Cooking Time: 5 minutes | Serving 2 | Difficulty: Easy)

Ingredients:

- 2 teaspoons olive oil
- ¼ cup Kalamata olives, chopped
- 1 clove garlic
- Ground black pepper and salt, to taste
- 1 ½ pounds leg of lamb in steaks
- 1 tablespoon lemon juice
- 2 teaspoons capers

Instructions:

1. Spray nonstick cooking spray in a big, heavy skillet and heat it to medium-high.

2. Slice the lamb steaks' edges while cooking to prevent curling. Add the oil to the hot skillet, and then add the steaks. They should be blackened on both sides.

3. Add the capers, lemon juice, garlic, and olives, to the steaks after they have been grilled on both sides. Allow everything to boil for another minute or 2, but avoid overcooking the lamb; it should remain pink in the center.

4. The steaks are seasoned with pepper and salt, divided into 4 parts, and served with all of the delicious lemon-caper-olive sauce scraped over them from the pan.

Nutritional Info: 483 cal, 42g fat (16g sag. fat), 108mg chol, 968mg sod, 3.4g carb (1.1g sugars, 1.7g fiber), 21.3g pro.

Spareribs Adobado

(Preparation Time: 5 minutes | Cooking Time: 2 hours | Serving 2 | Difficulty: Easy)

Ingredients:

- 4 tablespoons divided olive oil
- 1 tablespoon paprika, smoked
- 1 teaspoon oregano, dried
- ½ teaspoon black pepper, ground
- ½ cup chicken broth
- 3 divided cloves garlic
- 3 pounds pork spareribs
- 1 teaspoon cumin, ground
- ½ teaspoon salt

Instructions:

1. 2 garlic cloves should be crushed, and then 1 tablespoon of olive oil should be added.

2. Give it ten minutes to rest. Then, cover both sides of the ribs with this mixture by rubbing it on with clean hands. In a roasting pan, place them.

3. The spices should be mixed in a small bowl. Take 1 tablespoon of mixture, and reserve it in a small bowl.

4. The spice combination you didn't save in the bowl should be evenly distributed over the ribs. Include every aspect. Set the timer for 25 minutes and place the ribs in the oven to cook.

5. Crush the last garlic clove and combine it with the saved spice combination, chicken stock, and the leftover 3 tablespoons of olive oil while the ribs are roasting. To blend, stir. This sauce is for mopping.

6. When your timer goes off, flip the ribs and baste them with the mopping sauce. Set

your timer for 20 more minutes and place them again in the oven.

7. Repeat for 1 to 2 hours; the ribs should be sizzling, golden brown, and tender when poked with a fork. To serve, separate the ribs into pieces.

Nutritional Info: 157 cal, 8g fat (3g sag. fat), 60mg chol, 611mg sod, 1.6g carb (0.3g sugars, 0.2g fiber), 19g pro.

Roman Lamb Steak

(Preparation Time: 5 minutes | Cooking Time: 36 minutes | Serving 2 | Difficulty: Easy)

Ingredients:

- ½ cup fresh parsley, chopped
- 1 tablespoon lemon juice
- 1/8 teaspoon salt
- 1 crushed clove garlic
- ¾ pound leg of lamb steaks
- 1 tablespoon olive oil
- ¼ teaspoon black pepper, ground
- 2 anchovy fillets

Instructions:

1. Place the lamb steak on the platter. Place the S-blade in the food processor and add the other ingredients. Pulse several times to combine the anchovies, parsley, and garlic into a fine paste. Spread half of the resultant mixture over the steak's first side, flip it over and spread the remaining mixture on the second side. Let the steak rest now for at least 30 minutes.

2. After marinating, warm your broiler, then broil the lamb for 6 minutes on each side or until it is still pink in the center. Then, serve.

Nutritional Info: 241 cal, 17g fat (7g sag. fat), 82mg chol, 58mg sod, 0g carb (0g sugars, 0g fiber), 21g pro.

BANH MI Burgers

(Preparation Time: 5 minutes | Cooking Time: 10 minutes | Serving 2 | Difficulty: Easy)

Ingredients:

- ¼ cup basil leaves, fresh
- 1 tablespoon fish sauce
- 1 tablespoon Splenda
- 1 teaspoon salt
- 1/3 cup mayonnaise
- 5 divided scallions
- 1 pound pork, ground
- 1 tablespoon chili garlic sauce
- 2 teaspoons garlic, chopped
- 1 teaspoon black pepper, ground
- 1 tablespoon chili garlic sauce

Instructions:

1. Throw three scallions into the food processor after trimming the root or any limp leaves off of them. Include the basil as well. Pulse them together until they are well chopped.

2. Afterwards, add the pork to the processor along with the fish sauce, splenda, chili garlic sauce, salt, garlic, and pepper, and process until it is all combined.

3. Three patties made from the pork mixture are grilled. Place a six to eight-minute timer.

4. Reassemble your food processor with the S-blade in place after quickly cleaning it out. Add the last two scallions and pulse a few times to chop them. Next, stir in the mayonnaise and chili sauce.

5. Serve the burgers with the sauce after they are done.

Nutritional Info: 889 cal, 71g fat (24g sag. fat), 130mg chol, 940mg sod, 41g carb (1g sugars, 2g fiber), 28g pro.

Festive Pork

(Preparation Time: 5 minutes | Cooking Time: 5 minutes | Serving 2 | Difficulty: Easy)

Ingredients:

- 1 tablespoon vegetable or olive oil
- 2 tablespoons cranberries, dried
- 1 tablespoon orange juice concentrate
- ¾ lb. trimmed pork tenderloin

- ½ cup beef broth, low-sodium divided
- 1 ½ teaspoons Dijon mustard
- 1 teaspoon cornstarch

Instructions:

1. In a skillet on medium heat, brown in oil. When the meat is no pinker, add 1/4 cup of beef stock, cover, and simmer for about 5 to 10 minutes.

2. Put the meat on a serving platter and keep it heated.

3. The remaining stock, mustard, and cranberries are added to the pan.

4. Cornstarch and orange juice concentrate should be well combined before being added to the broth mixture while continually stirring. Continue cooking for one to two minutes after bringing it to a boil. Add to the pork.

Nutritional Info: 162 cal, 7g fat (5g sag. fat), 50mg chol, 210mg sod, 5g carb (16g sugars, 11g fiber), 92g pro.

One Pot Dinner

(Preparation Time: 5 minutes | Cooking Time: 25 minutes | Serving 2 | Difficulty: Easy)

Ingredients:

- 1 onion, medium chopped
- ¾ cup green pepper, chopped
- 1 tsp. Salt
- ¼ tsp. pepper
- 16 oz. tin kidney beans drained and rinsed
- ¾ cup water
- ½ lb. lean ground beef
- 1 cup celery, chopped
- 2 tsp. Worcestershire sauce
- ½ tsp. basil, dried
- 2 cups uncooked egg noodles, no-yolk medium
- 14 ½ oz. tin stewed tomatoes, no salt added
- 1 beef bouillon cube, low-sodium

Instructions:

1. Cook the beef in a big skillet or saucepan until it's no longer pink, then drain. Cook for 5 minutes, or until the veggies are crisp-tender, before adding the onion, celery, and green pepper.

2. Add the basil, pepper, Worcestershire sauce, and salt if preferred. Noodles, water, tomatoes, beans, and bouillon are all stirred up to a boil. Turn down the heat, cover the pot, and boil the noodles for twenty minutes, stirring periodically.

Nutritional Info: 282 cal, 5g fat (4g sag. fat), 29mg chol, 91mg sod, 39g carb (26g sugars, 18g fiber), 91g pro.

Chapter 5: Fish and Seafood Recipes

This chapter includes fish and various seafood recipes.

Glazed Salmon

(Preparation Time: 5 minutes | Cooking Time: 7 minutes | Serving 2 | Difficulty: Easy)

Ingredients:

- 3 tablespoons melted bacon grease
- 2 tablespoons brown mustard
- 1 tablespoon erythritol
- 1 ½ pounds salmon fillet
- Ground black pepper and salt, for taste
- 2 tablespoons horseradish, grated

Instructions:

1. Apply bacon grease to both sides of your fish. Add a little pepper and salt for seasoning.

2. Combine the remaining ingredients, and then have it ready.

3. Give your fish three minutes on the grill or broiler pan. Grill for 3 minutes on the opposite side after flipping. Apply the glaze now, flip it over and repeat on the other side. Give it a minute more, and then remove it off the grill to serve with any left glaze.

Nutritional Info: 403 cal, 23g fat (6g sag. fat), 89mg chol, 189mg sod, 22g carb (22g sugars, 0g fiber), 27g pro.

Cioppino

(Preparation Time: 5 minutes | Cooking Time: 5 minutes | Serving 2 | Difficulty: Easy)

Ingredients:

- 1 chopped onions
- ½ bunch of fresh chopped parsley
- ½ cups chicken broth
- ½ tbsp. basil, dried
- ¼ tsp. oregano, dried
- ½ cup white wine
- ½ pound bay scallops
- 6 mussels, debearded and cleaned
- ½ pounds cubed cod fillets
- ¼ cup coconut oil
- 1 minced cloves garlic
- ½ cup tomatoes, stewed
- 1 bay leaf
- ¼ tsp. thyme, dried
- ½ cup water
- ½ pound large shrimp, deveined and peeled
- 6 clams, small
- ½ cups crabmeat

Instructions:

1. Onions, garlic, and parsley are added to a large stockpot of melted coconut oil over medium heat. When onions are tender, cook them moderately while stirring periodically. To the saucepan, add tomatoes. Add wine, water, chicken broth, bay leaves, oregano, thyme, and basil. Mix thoroughly. For 30 minutes, simmer covered.

2. Add the crabmeat, shrimp, clams, scallops, and mussels by stirring. Stir in the fish.

3. Heating to a boil, reduce heat, cover, and let cook until clams open.

Nutritional Info: 380 cal, 16g fat (9g sag. fat), 219mg chol, 1728mg sod, 11g carb (4g sugars, 2.2g fiber), 40g pro.

Citrus Vinaigrette Salmon

(Preparation Time: 5 minutes | Cooking Time: 10 minutes | Serving 2 | Difficulty: Easy)

Ingredients:

- 1 ½ pounds salmon fillet
- ½ cup lemon juice
- 2 tablespoons lime juice
- 1 teaspoon chili powder
- 1 tablespoon coconut oil
- ½ cup vinaigrette
- 2 ½ tablespoons Splenda
- 1 teaspoon brown mustard
- ¼ teaspoon orange extract

Instructions:

1. Put a large skillet over medium heat after spraying it with nonstick cooking spray. The coconut oil should be added, melted, and then the salmon should be added.

2. Put everything else into the blender, and then run until the salmon becomes light gold.

3. Go ahead and flip the salmon now. Let the other side also turn a bit gold.

4. Turn the flame to medium-high and pour the vinaigrette mixture into the pan. Cook everything for five minutes or until the salmon is fully cooked.

5. Turn on the stove after plating the fish. The sauce should be hard-boiling until it has reduced and begun to become somewhat syrupy. Serve the salmon with the liquid.

Nutritional Info: 334 cal, 16g fat (4g sag. fat), 60mg chol, 290mg sod, 22g carb (15g sugars, 5g fiber), 27g pro.

Orange Coconut Oil Flounder

(Preparation Time: 5 minutes | Baking Time: 15 minutes | Serving 2 | Difficulty: Easy)

Ingredients:

- 1 tbsp. white wine
- 1 tbsp. coconut oil
- 1/3 tsp. black pepper
- ¼ tsp. salt
- 1 pound flounder
- 1 tbsp. lemon juice
- 1 tbsp. parsley
- 1 tbsp. orange zest
- ¼ cup scallions, chopped

Instructions:

1. Set the oven to 325°F. Add salt and pepper to the fish.

2. Inside the baking dish put the fish. Over the fish, sprinkle some orange zest.

3. Melt the leftover coconut oil, and then stir in the herbs and scallions before pouring it over the flounder. White wine is then added.

4. Bake for about 15 minutes after placing in the oven. Serve the excess liquid with the fish.

Nutritional Info: 130 cal, 7g fat (2g sag. fat), 30mg chol, 300mg sod, 9g carb (2g sugars, 1g fiber), 9g pro.

Deviled Pollock

(Preparation Time: 5 minutes | Cooking Time: 20 minutes | Serving 2 | Difficulty: Easy)

Ingredients:

- 2 tablespoons brown mustard
- 4 teaspoons Heinz Ketchup, without sugar
- 1 pound 6 Pollock fillets
- 2 tablespoons horseradish, prepared
- ½ teaspoon Sriracha

Instructions:

1. Lay your fillets in a shallow baking dish sprayed with nonstick cooking spray.

2. Combine the ketchup, mustard, Sriracha, and horseradish in a bowl. This mixture should be uniformly applied to the fish's surface.

3. Serve the fish after baking it for twenty minutes or until it flakes easily.

Nutritional Info: 100 cal, 1.1g fat (0.1g sag. fat), 77mg chol, 94mg sod, 0g carb (0g sugars, 0g fiber), 21g pro.

Grilled Salmon

(Preparation Time: 5 minutes | Cooking Time: 5 minutes | Serving 2 | Difficulty: Easy)

Ingredients:

- 2 tbsp. coconut oil
- 1 tbsp. lemon juice
- 1 minced clove garlic
- ¼ tsp. red pepper flakes, crushed
- 1/8 tsp. salt
- 2 salmon filets
- 1 tbsp. fish sauce
- 1 tbsp. Green onion, thinly sliced
- ¼ tsp. Ginger, ground
- ¼ tsp. sesame oil

Instructions:

1. Coconut oil, garlic, fish sauce, ginger, red chili flakes, green onions, lemon juice, salt, and sesame oil should all be combined in a bowl. Place the fish inside a glass dish and cover it with the marinade. For four hours, cover and chill.

2. Heat the grill. Salmon on the grill. Grill the salmon until it is tender.

3. Cooking while rotating halfway.

Nutritional Info: 468 cal, 28g fat (5g sag. fat), 143mg chol, 138mg sod, 0g carb (0g sugars, 0g fiber), 50g pro.

Portobello and Sun-Dried Tomato Salmon Roast

(Preparation Time: 5 minutes | Cooking Time: 5 minutes | Serving 2 | Difficulty: Easy)

Ingredients:

- 2 tablespoons sun-dried tomatoes, chopped
- 3 teaspoons divided olive oil
- 1 ounce sliced provolone cheese
- 2 tablespoons boiling water
- 8 ounces salmon fillet, 2 pieces
- ¼ cup Portobello mushrooms, sliced
- 1 teaspoon fresh parsley, minced

Instructions:

1. The chopped sun-dried tomatoes should be covered with boiling water. If your salmon has skin, use a small knife to remove it while allowing them to settle.

2. Use nonstick cooking spray to coat a small pan, and then add 2 tablespoons of olive oil. The mushrooms should be sautéed until they mellow and change color.

3. Now place one of your salmon fillet slabs on a baking sheet lined with nonstick foil or sprayed with nonstick cooking spray. Place the salmon fillet on top of the provolone. Make one layer of the tomatoes after draining any extra water.

4. Then add the mushrooms on top. The second salmon piece should now be placed on top.

5. To hold the layers together, pierce with a few skewers or toothpicks.

6. The final teaspoon of olive oil should be used to baste your salmon roast. Add some parsley to the dish. Please put it in the oven for the next twenty to thirty minutes.

7. To serve, cut the layers in half through layers.

Nutritional Info: 267 cal, 8g fat (1g sag. fat), 38mg chol, 227mg sod, 29g carb (3g sugars, 4g fiber), 19g pro.

Crab Cakes

(Preparation Time: 5 minutes | Cooking Time: 8 minutes | Serving 2 | Difficulty: Easy)

Ingredients:

- 1 egg, beaten
- 1 tbsp. mustard

- ¼ cup coconut oil
- 1 tbsp. lemon juice
- ¼ tsp. cayenne pepper
- 1 lb. crabmeat
- 1 cup flax seeds meal
- 1 tbsp. Horseradish, grated
- ½ tsp. lemon rind
- 1 tbsp. parsley
- 1 tsp. fish sauce

Instructions:

1. Combine all the ingredients except the oil in a medium bowl. Create smaller hamburger shapes.

2. Cook patties on each side for three to four minutes, or until golden brown, in a frying pan. You may bake them inside the oven if you like.

Nutritional Info: 250 cal, 11g fat (4g sag. fat), 5mg chol, 210mg sod, 30g carb (16g sugars, 11g fiber), 9g pro.

Transcendent Flounder

(Preparation Time: 5 minutes | Cooking Time: 10 minutes | Serving 2 | Difficulty: Easy)

Ingredients:

- 2 pounds of flounder fillets
- 1/3 cup mayonnaise
- 4 scallions
- ¼ cup butter
- 2 lemons
- 1/3 cup Parmesan cheese, grated

Instructions:

1. Start your broiler, and then position a rack 4 inches underneath it.

2. Melt the butter in a glass measuring cup or custard cup and microwave it for one minute.

3. Your broiler pan should be covered with foil and nonstick cooking spray. Give the edges a slight cup. Presently, arrange the flounder fillets. Use the brush or the back of the spoon to ensure the fillets are

uniformly covered after spreading the butter over them. Lemons should be cut in half, the seeds removed, and the liquid squeezed over the fish.

4. The fish should be placed on the broiler. Combine the mayonnaise and Parmesan as it cooks.

5. Your fillets should be almost finished now; it doesn't take long. Turn your pan and give them another minute to cook if they're browning unevenly. Spread this mayonnaise mixture evenly over the flounder until it starts to get opaque and flaky. Then, place them back underneath the broiler.

6. Your scallions into thin slices. Once again, inspect your fish; if the topping is browning unevenly, tilt the pan to make it even and cook for an additional minute or two.

7. Plate the fish, top each dish with sliced scallion, and serve once the topping is equally browned.

Nutritional Info: 109 cal, 3g fat (1g sag. fat), 71mg chol, 461mg sod, 0g carb (0g sugars, 0g fiber), 19g pro.

Pesto Mayonnaise Salmon

(Preparation Time: 5 minutes | Cooking Time: 7 minutes | Serving 2 | Difficulty: Easy)

Ingredients:

- ¼ cup mayonnaise
- 4 tablespoons Parmesan cheese, shredded
- 1 ½ pounds salmon fillet
- 4 teaspoons pesto sauce

Instructions:

1. It would help to place your salmon fillet's skin inside a shallow baking pan coated with nonstick cooking spray. Broil the salmon for four to five minutes at low heat, about 4 inches from the heat source.

2. Combine the pesto sauce and mayonnaise in the meanwhile. Spread the salmon with the pesto mayonnaise once the first broiling period has ended. Add 1 tablespoon of Parmesan cheese to each dish. Return the dish to the broiler for

approximately 1 ½ more minutes, just when the cheese begins to brown.

Nutritional Info: 92 cal, 3g fat (0g sag. fat), 41mg chol, 53mg sod, 0g carb (0g sugars, 0g fiber), 16g pro.

Dill Poached Trout

(Preparation Time: 5 minutes | Cooking Time: 5 minutes | Serving 2 | Difficulty: Easy)

Ingredients:

- 1 tablespoon lemon juice
- 12 ounces trout fillet
- 2 tablespoons dry white wine
- 1 tablespoon snipped dill weed, fresh or dried
- Ground black pepper and salt, for taste

Instructions:

1. Lemon juice and wine should be combined in a small, lidded pan that is not reactive. Place over medium heat, and then simmer. Lay the fish fillets skin-side up inside the wine-lemon juice mixture after stirring in the dill. Establish a timer over 8 minutes; lower the heat to low, and cover the pan.

2. Turn the trout fillets' skin-side down as you move them to two serving dishes. Sprinkle them with a little salt and pepper, then pour your pan liquid onto them and serve.

Nutritional Info: 124 cal, 6g fat (1.5g sag. fat), 45mg chol, 270mg sod, 0.3g carb (0.1g sugars, 0g fiber), 16g pro.

Pesto Shrimp

(Preparation Time: 5 minutes | Cooking Time: 5 minutes | Serving 2 | Difficulty: Easy)

Ingredients:

- 3 tablespoons pesto sauce
- 1 ½ tablespoons olive oil
- 18 ounces of shrimp, deveined and peeled

Instructions:

1. Over medium-high heat, combine pesto and olive oil in a large, heavy pan. When it's heated, add the shrimp and cook them until they are completely pink.

2. Scrape all of the pesto sauce out from the pan over them before serving.

Nutritional Info: 590 cal, 39g fat (9g sag. fat), 245mg chol, 3190mg sod, 25g carb (12g sugars, 8g fiber), 32g pro.

Halibut with Herb-Lemon Sauce

(Preparation Time: 5 minutes | Cooking Time: 5 minutes | Serving 2 | Difficulty: Easy)

Ingredients:

- 5 tablespoons olive oil, extra-virgin divided
- 3 tablespoons fresh parsley, chopped
- 1 kg halibut fillets
- 1 red bell pepper, medium rings sliced
- 6 tablespoons lemon juice
- 3 tablespoons fresh basil, chopped
- Ground black pepper and salt, for taste
- 3 tablespoons fresh chives, chopped

Instructions:

1. Set the broiler on high.

2. Place the S-blade on the food processor and add the basil, parsley, lemon juice, and 4 tablespoons of olive oil. Until puréed, pulse.

3. To taste, add pepper and salt to the food.

4. Pepper and gently salt the halibut fillets before brushing them with 1 tablespoon of oil left over. For just opaque through, broil for about 5 minutes on each side. Place on serving trays. Place the pepper rings over the sauce after scattering your chives over the fish and serving.

Nutritional Info: 217 cal, 11g fat (2g sag. fat), 65mg chol, 447mg sod, 1g carb (0g sugars, 0g fiber), 27g pro.

Moroccan Sizzling Shrimp

(Preparation Time: 5 minutes | Cooking Time: 8 minutes | Serving 2 | Difficulty: Easy)

Ingredients:

- 1 pound shrimp, deveined and peeled

- 2 teaspoons paprika
- ½ teaspoon ginger, ground
- 2 minced cloves garlic
- 1 tablespoon olive oil
- 2 teaspoons lemon juice
- 1 teaspoon cumin, ground
- 1/8 teaspoon cayenne

Instructions:

1. Put a big, heavy skillet over high heat after spraying it with nonstick cooking spray. Add the shrimp and the olive oil after it is heated. Turning often, sauté until they start to turn pink all over.

2. Add the additional ingredients, cook for another minute or two until the shrimp are completely pink, and then serve.

Nutritional Info: 572 cal, 11g fat (2.4g sag. fat), 0mg chol, 0mg sod, 91g carb (28g sugars, 15g fiber), 30g pro.

Gingered Monkfish

(Preparation Time: 5 minutes | Cooking Time: 10 minutes | Serving 2 | Difficulty: Easy)

Ingredients:

- 1 tablespoon fresh ginger root, grated
- 2 teaspoons Sriracha or chili garlic paste
- 3 scallions
- 1 teaspoon sesame oil, dark
- 1 pound monkfish
- 1 tablespoon Heinz Ketchup, without sugar
- 6 ounces asparagus, thinly speared
- 1 tablespoon coconut oil, peanut oil, or MCT oil

Instructions:

1. The monkfish should have any membrane removed using a sharp knife before being sliced into thin, flat, rounded slices. Reserve.

2. Combine the ketchup, ginger root, and chili garlic paste in a small bowl.

3. Apply this mixture to the slices of monkfish. Give it five minutes to sit.

4. Meanwhile, cut the asparagus ends where it naturally tries to break. On the diagonal, trim the spears to lengths of 1 inch. Also, cut your scallions into slices, paying attention to the crisp green portion.

5. Use a wok if you have one for this. If not, use your big, heavy skillet; just be sure to put nonstick cooking spray on it first. In any case, heat it and add your peanut oil.

6. Add the asparagus, scallion, and monkfish along with its sauce. Stir-fry the fish very carefully to avoid breaking it up. Cook for almost 5 minutes; to ensure that the veggies are crisp-tender and the fish is fully cooked.

7. Add the sesame oil, stir to blend, and then serve.

Nutritional Info: 433 cal, 24g fat (14g sag. fat), 48mg chol, 739mg sod, 21g carb (4.8g sugars, 1g fiber), 31g pro.

Baked Clams

(Preparation Time: 5 minutes | Cooking Time: 5 minutes | Serving 2 | Difficulty: Easy)

Ingredients:

- ¼ cup pork rind crumbs, plain
- 1 tablespoon fresh parsley, minced
- ½ teaspoon Tabasco sauce
- 36 clams inside shell
- ½ cup butter
- 2 tablespoons onion, minced
- 1 teaspoon oregano, dried
- 4 crushed cloves of garlic

Instructions:

1. Once thoroughly combined, process everything in the food processor except the clams.

2. Add a spoonful of this mixture to each clam at this point. In a baking pan, arrange. You may cover them, put them in the refrigerator, or freeze them.

3. Allow them to come to ambient temperature before cooking them.

4. Bake for about 10 minutes with the oven at 375°F, then broil, about 4 inches from the fire, for an additional three to five minutes or until brown. Serve warm

Nutritional Info: 39 cal, 2g fat (0.3g sag. fat), 0mg chol, 121mg sod, 1g carb (0.9g sugars, 0.1g fiber), 4.2g pro.

Bacon-Chili Scallops

(Preparation Time: 5 minutes | Cooking Time: 5 minutes | Serving 2 | Difficulty: Easy)

Ingredients:

- 2 teaspoons chili powder
- 8 slices bacon
- 1 pound bay scallops

Instructions:

1. Slice the bacon into pieces that are approximately ¼ inch wide and place the bacon in your big, heavy pan over medium heat. Fry that up.

2. Sprinkle the chili powder liberally over the scallops.

3. Add your scallops to the pan and spread them into a single layer when the bacon pieces are almost halfway done. The bacon pieces should be crisp, and the potatoes should be cooked through after approximately 5 minutes of cooking. Place the grease on top and serve with the bacon pieces.

Nutritional Info: 87 cal, 6.1g fat (2g sag. fat), 22mg chol, 923mg sod, 1.3g carb (0g sugars, 0.1g fiber), 6.7g pro.

Shrimp Scampi

(Preparation Time: 5 minutes | Cooking Time: 10 minutes | Serving 2 | Difficulty: Easy)

Ingredients:

- 1 ¾ cup chicken broth, low-sodium

- ¼ tsp. lemon and pepper seasoning, salt-free
- ¼ cup fresh parsley, minced and divided
- 8 oz. angel hair pasta
- 2 minced garlic cloves
- ¼ cup green onions, chopped and divided
- 1 lb. shrimp, uncooked, deveined and peeled

Instructions:

1. As directed on the box, cook the pasta.

2. Meanwhile, mix the broth, garlic, lemon-pepper spice, and 3 tablespoons each of green onions and parsley in a large pot. Up to a boil.

3. Cook for three to five minutes, or until shrimp become pink, after adding the shrimp. Put the spaghetti in a serving dish after draining. Add the shrimp mixture, the remaining onions, and the parsley.

Nutritional Info: 250 cal, 2g fat (1g sag. fat), 136mg chol, 398mg sod, 33g carb (15g sugars, 9g fiber), 23g pro.

Chapter 6: Soups Recipes

Asparagus and Crab Soup

(Preparation Time: 5 minutes | Cooking Time: 10 minutes | Serving 2 | Difficulty: Easy)

Ingredients:

- 2 teaspoons fresh ginger root, grated
- 2 eggs
- 1 tablespoon soy sauce
- 12 ounces lump crabmeat, tin or fresh
- 2 quarts chicken broth
- 1 pound asparagus
- 1 ½ tablespoons dry sherry
- 2 teaspoons sesame oil, dark

Instructions:

1. Start warming the broth in a big, heavy pot over medium heat. Add the ginger root and stir.

2. Now cut the asparagus ends where it naturally wants to break.

3. Slice the asparagus into 1/2-inch slices on the diagonal, discarding the ends. Add your asparagus to the soup after it has begun to boil. For three minutes or so, let it boil.

4. Beat the eggs in a glass container until they are well-combined while that is going on.

5. Hold a fork and the cup of whisked egg in the second because the asparagus is just beginning to get tender-crisp. After adding an egg to the soup's surface, mix it with a fork. Repeat. To include all the eggs, it should take three or four additions. You now have beautiful egg drops!

6. Soy sauce, sherry, and sesame oil should all be combined. Add the crab at this point, stir once more, and simmer for five minutes or so until serving.

Nutritional Info: 320 cal, 18g fat (12g sag. fat), 110mg chol, 1460mg sod, 24g carb (4g sugars, 4g fiber), 16g pro.

Cream of Salmon Soup

(Preparation Time: 5 minutes | Cooking Time: 10 minutes | Serving 2 | Difficulty: Easy)

Ingredients:

- ¼ cup onion, finely minced
- 2 cups heavy cream
- ½ teaspoon thyme, dried
- 1 ½ tablespoons butter
- ¼ cup celery, finely minced
- 390 g 1 tin salmon, drained

Instructions:

1. Melt the butter in a large pot over low heat before adding the onion and celery. The veggies should be sautéed for several minutes or until the onion becomes transparent.

2. Meanwhile, pour your cream into a 2-cup glass measuring cup or any comparable-sized microwaveable container with a spilling spout. It should be heated in the microwave for three to four minutes at 50% power.

3. The fish and thyme are then added to the pot with the cream. As you mix the soup, mash the fish. Serve after simmering for a moment.

Nutritional Info: 257.9 cal, 12.6g fat (3.3g sag. fat), 74.4mg chol, 1433mg sod, 6.4g carb (0.8g sugars, 0g fiber), 27.9g pro.

California Soup

(Preparation Time: 5 minutes | Cooking Time: 0 minutes | Serving 2 | Difficulty: Easy)

Ingredients:

- 1-quart chicken broth, hot
- 2 small or 1 large avocado, very ripe

Instructions:

1. The avocado should be peeled, pitted, and chopped into large pieces.

2. Blend the broth in a blender until completely smooth; take care while combining hot liquids. Then, serve.

Nutritional Info: 150 cal, 6g fat (3.5g sag. fat), 20mg chol, 1230mg sod, 18g carb (8g sugars, 1g fiber), 5g pro.

Tuna Chinese-Style Soup

(Preparation Time: 5 minutes | Cooking Time: 5 minutes | Serving 2 | Difficulty: Easy)

Ingredients:

- 2 teaspoons soy sauce
- 2 eggs
- 1 ½ cups fresh spinach, chopped
- 1-quart chicken broth
- 1 teaspoon fresh ginger root, grated
- 170 g 1 tin tuna in olive oil
- 2 scallions, thinly sliced

Instructions:

1. Combine the chicken broth and ginger in a large pot. Please boil over medium-high heat, and then reduce the heat so that the broth is gently simmering.

2. Break your eggs into a small glass measuring cup or any container having a pouring lip while the broth is cooking. Use a fork to batter them. Pour one-third of your egg into the boiling soup, wait only a few seconds, and then mix with a fork to separate the egg into strands. Repeat in two or three more additions with the remaining egg.

3. Add the spinach and tuna after the egg has been added. Heat thoroughly, then garnish with scallions.

Nutritional Info: 70.8 cal, 0.6g fat (0.4g sag. fat), 5.7mg chol, 169mg sod, 9.7g carb (5.9g sugars, 1.8g fiber), 5.6g pro.

Stracciatella

(Preparation Time: 5 minutes | Cooking Time: 5 minutes | Serving 2 | Difficulty: Easy)

Ingredients:

- 2 eggs
- ½ teaspoon lemon juice
- ½ teaspoon marjoram, dried

- 1 quart divided chicken broth
- ½ cup Parmesan cheese, grated
- 1 pinch of nutmeg, ground

Instructions:

1. In a small pitcher or glass measuring cup, pour 1/4 cup of the broth. Over medium heat, add the remaining ingredients to a big saucepan.

2. Beat the eggs with a fork and add them to the measuring cup of broth. The Parmesan, nutmeg, and lemon juice are added, and everything is well mixed with a fork.

3. Whenever the broth inside the saucepan is boiling, add a little bit of the egg and cheese mixture at a time and whisk it all together with a fork.

4. Before serving, let the soup a final minute or two of simmering after adding the marjoram and giving it a little squeeze between your fingers.

Nutritional Info: 80 cal, 7g fat (4.5g sag. fat), 25mg chol, 140mg sod, 0g carb (0g sugars, 0g fiber), 3g pro.

Tavern Soup

(Preparation Time: 5 minutes | Cooking Time: 15 minutes | Serving 2 | Difficulty: Easy)

Ingredients:

- ¼ cup celery, finely diced
- ¼ cup carrot, shredded
- ½ teaspoon black pepper, ground
- 12 ounces of light beer
- ¼ teaspoon hot pepper sauce
- 1 ½ quarts chicken broth
- ¼ cup green bell pepper, finely diced
- ¼ cup fresh parsley, chopped
- 1 pound Cheddar cheese, sharp shredded
- ½ teaspoon salt
- Xanthan or guar, as required

Instructions:

1. In the cooker, mix the celery, carrot, green pepper, parsley, & black pepper with the liquid. For 6 to 8 minutes of cooking, at high.

2. When cooking is over, either use a hand blender to puree the veggies directly in the cooker or remove them using a slotted spoon, puree them in your blender and then put them in.

3. Once the cheese has completely melted in, add it gradually by whisking. Stir in the beer, salt, and spicy sauce when the foam has subsided. Use guar to thicken the soup until it consistently resembles heavy cream.

Nutritional Info: 100 cal, 0g fat (0g sag. fat), 0mg chol, 25mg sod, 27g carb (4g sugars, 12g fiber), 9g pro.

Egg Drop Soup

(Preparation Time: 5 minutes | Cooking Time: 6 minutes | Serving 2 | Difficulty: Easy)

Ingredients:

- ¼ teaspoon xanthan or guar (optional)
- 1 tablespoon rice vinegar
- 1 sliced scallion
- 1 quart divided chicken broth
- 1 tablespoon soy sauce
- ½ teaspoon fresh ginger root, grated
- 2 eggs

Instructions:

1. Turn your blender on low speed, add the guar, and pour about 1 cup of chicken broth. Please put it in a big pot with the leftover 3 cups of broth after blending for a little period.

2. Add the rice vinegar, scallion, ginger, soy sauce, and so on. Bring to a boil and simmer for about five minutes to let the flavors meld over medium-high heat.

3. Beat your eggs with a pouring lip in a glass container or small pitcher. Pour in approximately one-fourth of the eggs and stir as they boil and shred using a fork as you slowly swirl the top of the soup. Utilize

all of the eggs by repeating them three more times.

Nutritional Info: 66 cal, 1.5g fat (0.4g sag. fat), 56mg chol, 903mg sod, 10g carb (0.2g sugars, 1g fiber), 2.8g pro.

Not Pea Soup

(Preparation Time: 5 minutes | Cooking Time: 15 minutes | Serving 2 | Difficulty: Easy)

Ingredients:

- ½ cup onion, chopped
- 1 carrot, medium grated
- 441 g 4 tins green beans
- 2 bay leaves
- Ground black pepper and salt, for taste
- 3 tablespoons butter
- ½ cup celery, chopped
- 115 g 4 ounces ham
- ½ teaspoon thyme, dried
- 2 pinches of cayenne

Instructions:

1. Melt the butter in a large skillet over medium heat, and then begin sautéing the onion, carrot, and celery.

2. Add the ham to your food processor, attach the S-blade, and pulse until the meat is medium-finely minced. Scrape this into your saucepan with the vegetables after processing it in the food processor. While you're there, mix things up.

3. Put your S-blade back in the processor bowl and place it on the base. Add the green beans to the food processor and any liquid, and pulse till the beans are very smooth.

4. Please return to your sautéing veggies and add the garlic once they are tender. It should only be sautéed for one minute with the veggies.

5. Your green bean puree should now be added. Stir everything together. Stir in the bay leaves, thyme, and cayenne pepper. Simmer the soup for a little while on low heat. Allow it to cook for about fifteen minutes.

6. After removing the bay leaves and seasoning with pepper and salt, ladle the soup into glasses.

Nutritional Info: 158 cal, 2.8g fat (1.4g sag. fat), 0mg chol, 870mg sod, 26g carb (8.3g sugars, 4.9g fiber), 8.3g pro.

Mushroom Cream Soup

(Preparation Time: 5 minutes | Cooking Time: 10 minutes | Serving 2 | Difficulty: Easy)

Ingredients:

- ¼ cup onion, chopped
- 1-quart chicken broth
- ½ cup sour cream
- Xanthan or guar (optional)
- 8 ounces mushrooms, sliced
- 2 tablespoons butter
- ½ cup heavy cream
- Ground black pepper and salt, for taste

Instructions:

1. Sauté the onion and mushrooms in the butter in a large, heavy pan until the mushrooms mellow and change color. Please place them in the cooker. Put the broth in. For five to six minutes, cook the food in a cooker on high heat.

2. When the time is up, use a slotted spoon to remove the veggies and add them to your food processor or blender. Pour in enough broth to enable easy processing and fine purée. Refill the cooker with the puréed veggies, scooping out every last piece using a rubber scraper.

3. Now incorporate the sour cream and heavy cream, and season to taste with salt and pepper. If you believe it requires it, add some guar or xanthan gum to thicken it. Serve right away.

Nutritional Info: 410 cal, 23g fat (7g sag. fat), 25mg chol, 2249mg sod, 36g carb (18g sugars, 1.9g fiber), 15g pro.

Olive Soup

(Preparation Time: 5 minutes | Cooking Time: 5 minutes | Serving 2 | Difficulty: Easy)

Ingredients:

- ½ teaspoon xanthan or guar
- 1 cup heavy cream
- Ground black pepper and salt, for taste
- 1 quart divided chicken broth
- 100 g 1 cup black olives, minced
- ¼ cup dry sherry

Instructions:

1. Mix briefly with the guar and ½ cup of chicken broth inside the blender. Pour the leftover 3 ½ cups of broth plus the olives into a saucepan.

2. Stir in the cream after raising the heat to a simmer. Add the sherry, bring it back to a simmer, and add pepper and salt to taste.

Nutritional Info: 616 cal, 10g fat (0g sag. fat), 17.5mg chol, 175mg sod, 16g carb (0.5g sugars, 0.5g fiber), 5g pro.

Sopa Tlalpeño

(Preparation Time: 5 minutes | Cooking Time: 10 minutes | Serving 2 | Difficulty: Easy)

Ingredients:

- 1 pound chicken breast, skinless and boneless
- 1 Hass avocado
- Ground black pepper and salt, for taste
- 1 ½ quarts divided chicken broth
- 1 chipotle chile tin adobo
- 4 sliced scallions
- ¾ cup Monterey Jack cheese, shredded

Instructions:

1. Place a large, massive saucepan over medium-high heat and add the chicken stock, reserving ½ cup. Cut your chicken breast into thin strips or tiny cubes while the broth is cooking, then add them. Simmer everything for ten to fifteen minutes or when the chicken is well cooked.

2. Blend the chipotle in your blender with the saved chicken broth until the chipotle gets

puréed. Stir the soup after adding this combination.

3. Remove the seed from the avocado, peel it, and chop it into slices measuring ½ inch. Add the scallions, along with pepper and salt to taste, to the soup.

4. Pour the soup into bowls and sprinkle shredded cheese on each portion.

Nutritional Info: 271 cal, 10.1g fat (1.4g sag. fat), 31.3mg chol, 881mg sod, 26.7g carb (3.1g sugars, 4.7g fiber), 19.7g pro.

Cauliflower Purée

(Preparation Time: 3 minutes | Cooking Time: 12 minutes | Serving 2 | Difficulty: Easy)

Ingredients:

- 2 ounces of cream cheese
- Ground black pepper and salt, for taste
- 1 head cauliflower
- ¼ cup butter

Instructions:

1. Trim your cauliflower stem down, and then take the leaves off. Slice up the remaining food.

2. Put the cauliflower, a few tablespoons of water, and a lid on a microwave-safe casserole dish or the microwave steamer.

3. 12 minutes high in the microwave will get it pretty tender but not sulphur-smelling. Drain it completely. Puree it now.

4. Butter and cream cheese should be incorporated before adding pepper and salt to taste.

Nutritional Info: 204 cal, 17g fat (9.9g sag. fat), 44mg chol, 696mg sod, 9.8g carb (4.3g sugars, 4.6g fiber), 6.5g pro.

Vegetable Broth

(Preparation Time: 5 minutes | Cooking Time: 10 minutes | Serving 2 | Difficulty: Easy)

Ingredients:

- 1 onion, large
- 2 carrots, large

- 8 minced cloves garlic
- 6 sprigs thyme, fresh
- 1 tsp. salt
- 1 tbsp. coconut oil
- 2 stalks of celery, leaves
- 1 bunch of chopped green onions
- 8 sprigs parsley, fresh
- 2 bay leaves
- 2 quarts water

Instructions:

1. Cut vegetables into tiny pieces. Onion, celery, scallions, carrots, parsley, garlic, thyme, plus bay leaves are added to a soup pot that has been heated with oil. Stirring periodically, cook for five to seven minutes over high heat.

2. Add salt after bringing it to a boil. Reduce heat, cover, and simmer for 10 minutes.

3. Strain. Other items to think about are celery root and broccoli stem.

Nutritional Info: 17 cal, 0.2g fat (0g sag. fat), 0mg chol, 3180mg sod, 1.9g carb (1.1g sugars, 0g fiber), 2.1g pro.

Beef Broth

(Preparation Time: 5 minutes | Cooking Time: 15 minutes | Serving 2 | Difficulty: Easy)

Ingredients:

- 1 pound stew meat
- 2 onions, medium quartered and peeled
- 1 celery rib
- A handful of parsley, leaves and stems
- 10 peppercorns
- 5 pounds of beef bones
- Olive oil
- 2 carrots, large
- 3 unpeeled cloves of garlic
- 2 bay leaves

Instructions:

1. Beef should be added to a stockpot with cold water. Just bring it to a boil. Remove

any foam from the top by skimming. Add the other ingredients to a moderate simmer, and then quickly return to a boil. Cook for fifteen minutes on a high flame inside the cooker.

2. Strain after letting cool to a warm room temperature. Within a few days, utilize the broth or freeze it and keep it refrigerated. Defrost and cook food before using

Nutritional Info: 250 cal, 11g fat (4g sag. fat), 5mg chol, 210mg sod, 30g carb (16g sugars, 11g fiber), 9g pro.

Chicken Broth

(Preparation Time: 5 minutes | Cooking Time: 10 minutes | Serving 2 | Difficulty: Easy)

Ingredients:

- 2 onions, peeled
- 1 carrot
- 2 sprigs thyme, fresh
- 2 sprigs parsley, fresh
- 1 tsp. salt
- 4 lbs. chicken, fresh
- 2 celery stalks
- 8 black peppercorns

Instructions:

1. Chicken should be added to a stockpot with cold water. Just bring it to a boil. Remove any foam from the top by skimming. Add the other ingredients to a moderate simmer, and then quickly return to a boil. Cook for ten minutes on a high flame inside the cooker.

2. Strain after letting cool to a warm room temperature. Within a few days, utilize the broth or freeze it and keep it refrigerated. Defrost and cook food before using.

Nutritional Info: 15 cal, 1g fat (0g sag. fat), 0mg chol, 928mg sod, 0g carb (0g sugars, 0g fiber), 1g pro.

Tortellini Soup

(Preparation Time: 5 minutes | Cooking Time: 10 minutes | Serving 2 | Difficulty: Easy)

Ingredients:

- 1 minced garlic clove
- 8 oz. cheese tortellini
- 10 oz. 1 pkg. chopped frozen spinach, drained and thawed
- 1 onion, medium chopped
- 2 cup chicken broth, low-sodium
- 14 ½ oz. 1 tin Italian stewed tomatoes, salt-free

Instructions:

1. Garlic and onion should be sautéed until soft in a large pan with nonstick cooking spray. To boil, add the broth. Reduce heat before adding the tortellini.

2. Tortellini must be cooked for ten min or until soft. Add spinach and tomatoes and stir to combine.

Nutritional Info: 147 cal, 4g fat (1g sag. fat), 14mg chol, 186mg sod, 22g carb (13g sugars, 7g fiber), 8g pro.

Chapter 7: Snacks Recipes

Cajun Pecans

(Preparation Time: 5 minutes | Cooking Time: 10 minutes | Serving 2 | Difficulty: Easy)

Ingredients:

- 200 g or 2 cups pecan halves
- 30 g or 2 tablespoons of coconut oil
- 9 g or 1 tablespoon Creole seasoning

Instructions:

1. Set the oven to 350°F. Put your coconut oil inside a roasting pan and place it into the oven to melt while it's cooking.

2. Put your pecans in the pan after the oil has fully melted and swirl until they are evenly covered. Spread them out equally and re-bake the cookies. They have ten minutes.

3. After removing them from the oven and adding the Creole spice, let them cool.

4. Please keep it in an airtight package.

Nutritional Info: 190 cal, 16g fat (2g sag. fat), 0mg chol, 290mg sod, 12g carb (2g sugars, 4g fiber), 1g pro.

Cheese-Garlic Stuffed Mushrooms

(Preparation Time: 5 minutes | Cooking Time: 30 minutes | Serving 2 | Difficulty: Easy)

Ingredients:

- 170 g 1 package garlic plus spreadable herb cheese
- 6 Portobello mushrooms, small
- 2 tablespoons plain pork skins or rinds, crushed

Instructions:

1. Remove the stems from the mushrooms, and then clean them. Place some cheese into each mushroom cap. Add a teaspoon more pork rind crumbs to each one.

2. Put your mushrooms inside a baking dish that is not too deep. Just enough water should be added to film the pan's bottom. Bake for about 30 minutes, and then warmly serve.

Nutritional Info: 120 cal, 8g fat (5g sag. fat), 25mg chol, 340mg sod, 5g carb (1g sugars, 2g fiber), 5g pro.

Pepperoni Chips

(Preparation Time: 1 minute | Cooking Time: 2 minutes | Serving 2 | Difficulty: Easy)

Ingredients:

- 56 g or 2 ounces pepperoni slices

Instructions:

1. On a microwave-safe dish, place the pepperoni slices and microwave for sixty to ninety seconds or until crisp. That's it.

Nutritional Info: 145 cal, 11g fat (3.5g sag. fat), 30mg chol, 525mg sod, 0g carb (0g sugars, 0g fiber), 13g pro.

Chicken Tacos

(Preparation Time: 2 minutes | Cooking Time: 14 minutes | Serving 2 | Difficulty: Easy)

Ingredients:

- ¼ cup lime juice
- 1 tbsp. dried or fresh parsley, minced
- 1 tsp. oregano, dried
- 4 chicken breast halves, skinless and boneless
- 1/3 cup vegetable or olive oil
- 4 minced garlic cloves

- 1 tsp. Cumin, ground
- ½ tsp. pepper
- 2 flour tortillas, warmed

Instructions:

1. Combine the ingredients in a large, lockable plastic bag or a shallow glass jar. Chicken is added; turn to coat. Seal or cover, then chill for eight hours or overnight while periodically rotating. Drain and throw out the marinade.

2. Over medium heat, grill the chicken, uncovered, for five to seven minutes on each side or until the juices run clear.

3. Serve with chosen toppings in tortillas after being cut into thin strips.

Nutritional Info: 230 cal, 9g fat (2g sag. fat), 5mg chol, 350mg sod, 19g carb (2g sugars, 2g fiber), 18g pro.

Rosemary Walnuts

(Preparation Time: 5 minutes | Cooking Time: 8 minutes | Serving 2 | Difficulty: Easy)

Ingredients:

- 2 g or 2 teaspoons rosemary, ground
- 200 g or 2 cups walnuts
- 35 g or 2 ½ tablespoons coconut oil
- ¼ teaspoon cayenne
- Salt, for taste

Instructions:

1. Place the roasting pan containing the coconut oil inside the oven while it is preheating. The oil will melt in a few minutes.

2. After the oil has melted, pull out the pan, and add the cayenne and rosemary. They should be well mixed with coconut oil.

3. Walnuts will now be added to the pan. Spread them out in a uniform layer after thoroughly stirring to ensure that they are all covered with the seasoned oil. Re-enter the oven with the pan, and set the timer for five minutes.

Nutritional Info: 370 cal, 36g fat (3.5g sag. fat), 0mg chol, 135mg sod, 9g carb (2g sugars, 4g fiber), 9g pro.

Cheese Crackers

(Preparation Time: 1 minute | Cooking Time: 2 minutes | Serving 2 | Difficulty: Easy)

Ingredients:

- 4 American cheese slices

Instructions:

1. Lay the cheese on a microwaveable dish coated with nonstick cooking spray. For sixty to seventy-five seconds, microwave.

2. Peel it from the platter after letting it cool for about a minute. Before putting the cheese in the microwave, chop it into quarters if you want more cracker-like crackers.

Nutritional Info: 179 cal, 12g fat (6g sag. fat), 29mg chol, 281mg sod, 10g carb (2.3g sugars, 1g fiber), 7.9g pro.

Wicked Wings

(Preparation Time: 10 minutes | Cooking in the oven: 1 hour | Serving 2 | Difficulty: Easy)

Ingredients:

- 100 g or 1 cup Parmesan cheese, grated
- 1 tablespoon oregano, dried
- 1 teaspoon salt
- ½ cup butter
- 4 pounds of chicken wings
- 2 tablespoons parsley, dried
- 2 teaspoons paprika
- ½ teaspoon black pepper, ground

Instructions:

1. Set the oven to 350°F. Use foil to line a shallow baking pan.

2. Save the sharp tips for the broth and cut your wings onto single joints. Or not. You decide.

3. Mix the parsley, Parmesan cheese, oregano, salt, paprika, and pepper in a bowl.

4. Butter should be melted in a pan or shallow basin.

5. Then, roll each wing joint inside the cheese and spice mixture before placing it on the foil-lined pan.

6. After an hour of baking, curse yourself for not making a double batch!

Nutritional Info: 396 cal, 24g fat (4.7g sag. fat), 0mg chol, 194mg sod, 15g carb (1.4g sugars, 0.1g fiber), 21g pro.

Crab-Stuffed Mushrooms

(Preparation Time: 10 minutes | Cooking in the oven: 1 hour | Serving 2 | Difficulty: Easy)

Ingredients:

- 170 g 1 tin crab meat
- ¼ cup mayonnaise
- 12 minced scallions
- 1 dash of Tabasco sauce
- 1 pound of mushrooms, fresh
- 2 ounces of cream cheese
- ¼ cup Parmesan cheese, grated
- ¼ teaspoon black pepper, ground

Instructions:

1. Remove the stems and use a moist towel to clean the mushrooms.

2. Cream cheese, crabs, mayonnaise, scallions, Parmesan, Tabasco, and pepper should all be combined and mixed well in a mixing dish. After spooning the mixture into caps, place the mushroom caps on a large, wide roasting pan.

3. Bake the mushrooms for 45 to One hour or until they've completely cooked.

4. Serve warm.

Nutritional Info: 56 cal, 3.9g fat (2.3g sag. fat), 23mg chol, 80mg sod, 2.4g carb (0.5g sugars, 0.4g fiber), 2.6g pro.

Chicken Chips

(Preparation Time: 5 minutes | Cooking Time: 20 minutes | Serving 2 | Difficulty: Easy)

Ingredients:

- Salt, for taste

- 1 chicken skin

Instructions:

1. Set the oven to 350°F. Lay the skin of the chicken out flat on the broiler rack. Include any pieces of fat as well.

2. Bake them for at least twenty minutes until they are crisp and golden.

3. To taste, sprinkle them with salt.

Nutritional Info: 190 cal, 14g fat (3.5g sag. fat), 80mg chol, 470mg sod, 1g carb (0g sugars, 0g fiber), 13g pro.

Spanish Spicy Wings

(Preparation Time: 10 minutes | Cooking Time: 15 minutes | Serving 2 | Difficulty: Easy)

Ingredients:

- 1 tablespoon olive oil
- 1 tablespoon paprika
- 1 teaspoon salt
- ¼ teaspoon cayenne
- 3 cloves garlic, finely minced
- 8 chicken wings, large whole
- 1 teaspoon oregano, dried
- 1 teaspoon black pepper, ground
- 1 lime, wedges cut

Instructions:

1. To allow the taste of the garlic to permeate the oil, combine the garlic and olive oil and let them rest together for about ten minutes. Next, apply oil all over the wings.

2. Heat a broiler or grill in the meanwhile.

3. Mix the oregano, paprika, pepper, salt, and cayenne in a large basin. Add the wings and coat in the mixture.

4. The wings should be cooked all the way through, with crispy skin with a few blackened places, after 15 minutes on the grill or under the broiler. Garnish with lime wedges nearby for squeezing.

Nutritional Info: 219 cal, 7.2g fat (2.3g sag. fat), 46mg chol, 328mg sod, 18g carb (5g sugars, 1g fiber), 21g pro.

Cheese Nacho Crisps

(Preparation Time: 5 minutes | Cooking Time: 5 minutes | Serving 2 | Difficulty: Easy)

Ingredients:

- ½ teaspoon garlic powder
- ¼ teaspoon cayenne, more for taste
- 115 g or 1 cup Cheddar cheese, shredded without additives
- ½ teaspoon onion powder

Instructions:

1. Spray nonstick cooking spray on a microwaveable dish. Place approximately ¼ cup of the cheese on the dish and microwave it for two to three minutes on high or until it forms a crispy disc that resembles the orange on the moon's surface.
2. Allow it to cool for one or two minutes, then cook another batch after lifting it off the plate's surface with a knife.
3. Between batches, the plate needed to be repainted.

Nutritional Info: 147 cal, 7.8g fat (1.1g sag. fat), 5mg chol, 195mg sod, 17.2g carb (0.7g sugars, 1.4g fiber), 2.1g pro.

Deviled Eggs

(Preparation Time: 10 minutes | Cooking Time: 5 minutes | Serving 2 | Difficulty: Easy)

Ingredients:

- 2/3 cup mayonnaise
- 1 teaspoon Tabasco sauce
- Paprika
- 6 eggs, hard-boiled
- 1 tablespoon brown mustard
- Ground black pepper and salt, for taste

Instructions:

1. The yolks should be mixed with mustard, mayonnaise, and Tabasco. The mixture has to be processed until it reaches the desired consistency, scraping down the edges a few times.

2. To taste, add pepper and salt to the food.
3. Currently, add the yolks to the whites.
4. Add paprika to the top, then serve or chill.

Nutritional Info: 79 cal, 6.7g fat (1.5g sag. fat), 109mg chol, 80mg sod, 0.6g carb (0.1g sugars, 0.2g fiber), 3.7g pro.

Cinnamon-Butter Crispi's

(Preparation Time: 5 minutes | Cooking Time: 10 minutes | Serving 2 | Difficulty: Easy)

Ingredients:

- 30-45 g or 2-3 tablespoons erythritol, powdered
- 100 g or 3 ½ ounces plain skins or pork rinds
- 4 ½ g tablespoons Splenda
- 45 g or 3 tablespoons butter
- ¼ teaspoon cinnamon, ground
- 2 to 3 alternative sweeteners
- 6-9 g or 3 tablespoons Raw Stevia

Instructions:

1. Combine the cinnamon and erythritol powder in a small bowl.
2. It takes some perseverance, but after the butter has melted, add the pork rinds and stir until they are all uniformly coated.
3. Stirring continuously will help ensure that the erythritol-cinnamon mixture gets dispersed as evenly as feasible over the pork rinds.
4. Give the pan five minutes in the oven after sliding it in. Remove it and whisk it one more.
5. Five more and they'll be done.

Nutritional Info: 102.4 cal, 2.8g fat (0.7g sag. fat), 0mg chol, 250mg sod, 18.2g carb (5.2g sugars, 1.1g fiber), 2g pro.

Fish Eggs

(Preparation Time: 5 minutes | Cooking Time: 5 minutes | Serving 2 | Difficulty: Easy)

Ingredients:

- ¼ cup mayonnaise

- ½ cup moist salmon, smoked and finely mashed
- 4 teaspoons sweet red onion, finely minced
- 6 eggs, hard-boiled
- ¼ cup sour cream
- 2 tablespoons jarred horseradish, grated
- ¼ teaspoon salt

Instructions:

1. Cut the eggs in halves, gently scoop out the yolks and place them in a mixing dish.

2. With a fork, mash the yolks. Once everything is well combined and creamy, add the salmon, mayonnaise, horseradish, sour cream, salt, and onion.

3. Refill the egg white cavities with a portion of the mixture.

Nutritional Info: 104 cal, 2.9g fat (0.5g sag. fat), 439mg chol, 160mg sod, 4.9g carb (0g sugars, 0g fiber), 15g pro.

Stuffed Spinach Mushrooms

(Preparation Time: 5 minutes | Baking Time: 30 minutes | Serving 2 | Difficulty: Easy)

Ingredients:

- 2 tablespoons butter
- 4 cloves crushed garlic
- 4 ounces of cream cheese
- 1 ½ teaspoons Worcestershire sauce
- ¼ teaspoon black pepper, ground
- 1 ½ pounds mushroom
- ½ cup chopped onion
- 1 package chopped frozen spinach, thawed
- ¼ cup Parmesan cheese; add more for sprinkling
- ½ teaspoon salt

Instructions:

1. Remove the stems from the mushrooms and clean them. Cut the stems into pretty tiny pieces and set the caps aside.

2. Melt the butter in a large, sturdy pan over low heat. Add the onion and the chopped stems. These should be sautéed until the onion is transparent and the mushroom chunks start to change color. Mix in the garlic after adding the other ingredients for a few more minutes.

3. While that's going on, place your frozen spinach in a sieve and squeeze as much water as you can out of it. Add it to the mushroom-onion mixture at this time.

4. Add the cream cheese next and combine. Add the Parmesan cheese, Worcestershire sauce, pepper, and salt, after it has melted.

5. Fill the mushroom caps with the spinach-mushroom mixture. As you fill the caps, arrange them in a baking tray.

6. Add more Parmesan cheese to them after they are all filled to give them a good appearance. Just enough water should be added to cover the pan's bottom.

7. For 30 minutes, bake. Serve hot.

Nutritional Info: 44 cal, 3g fat (1g sag. fat), 10mg chol, 86mg sod, 2g carb (0.4g sugars, 0.6g fiber), 2g pro.

Chicken Meat Pizza

(Preparation Time: 5 minutes | Cooking Time: 35 minutes | Serving 2 | Difficulty: Easy)

Ingredients:

- ½ cup low-fat shredded cheddar
- Few basils leaves
- ½ cup chicken breast, minced and cooked
- ½ tbsp. Onion, minced
- ½ tsp. garlic, minced

Instructions:

1. The oven should be heated to 425 degrees. Together, chicken, onion, and garlic are processed. The mixture will have the texture of thick crumbs. On a baking sheet covered with parchment paper, press the chicken mixture. For 12 minutes, bake. Give it five minutes to cool.

2. Add 1/4 cup tomato sauce, a few low-fat cheese cubes, basil, and mushrooms on top (shiitake). Bake for 6 to 8 minutes or until the toppings are melted.

3. Give it five minutes to cool. Slice, then dish. As an alternative, you may wish to try the version with cauliflower crust:

4. The huge cauliflower should be grated and steamed for 15 minutes. Squeeze out the extra water, and then let it cool. Add two eggs, a cup of low-fat mozzarella, salt, and pepper. Create a 10-inch circular by patting the dough onto the baking sheet. Oil the baking sheet and bake till brown. As before, add the topping.

Nutritional Info: 382 cal, 20g fat (8g sag. fat), 39mg chol, 897mg sod, 33g carb (3g sugars, 2g fiber), 17g pro.

Chapter 8: Desserts Recipes

This chapter includes low-sugar dessert recipes.

Cheesecake

(Preparation Time: 5 minutes | Cooking Time: 15 minutes | Serving 2 | Difficulty: Easy)

Ingredients:

- 1 cups Splenda
- 2 eggs, big
- 1 pound cream cheese at room temperature
- 1 ½ tablespoons heavy cream

Instructions:

1. Turn on the 375°F oven.
2. Utilizing an electric mixer, fully combine everything. Spread in a 9-inch springform pan with butter.
3. For fifteen minutes, bake the cheesecake. Remove your cake and carefully run a knife along the pan's edge when the cake is done.
4. Place the cake back in the hot oven and leave it there until the oven has cooled.
5. Overnight in the refrigerator, then enjoy!

Nutritional Info: 401 cal, 28g fat (12g sag. fat), 69mg chol, 548mg sod, 32g carb (27g sugars, 0.5g fiber), 6.9g pro.

Glazed Walnuts

(Preparation Time: 5 minutes | Cooking Time: 5 minutes | Serving 2 | Difficulty: Easy)

Ingredients:

- Boiling water, as required
- 1 tablespoon erythritol
- 1 ½ cups walnut
- ½ teaspoon vanilla extract
- Coconut oil to fry

Instructions:

1. Place the walnuts in a basin and pour the boiling water over them. After just 4 or 5 minutes, drain them thoroughly.
2. Once the vanilla has been added, stir to distribute it evenly. When everything is well coated, add the erythritol and toss again. Your walnuts should now be spread out on a platter and let dry for a few hours. Spitting will be reduced when you fry them as a result.
3. Add ¼ inch of coconut oil to a large, heavy skillet on medium heat. Let it heat up, then fry the walnuts a few at a time until they are just beginning to crisp up. Cool, and then put it in a jar with a secure cover.

Nutritional Info: 190 cal, 14g fat (1g sag. fat), 0mg chol, 135mg sod, 12g carb (9g sugars, 1g fiber), 3g pro.

Cream Cheese Balls

(Preparation Time: 5 minutes | Cooking Time: 0 minutes | Serving 2 | Difficulty: Easy)

Ingredients:

- 8 ½ g 1 package gelatin, sugar-free, any flavor
- 8 ounces of chilled cream cheese

Instructions:

1. Your cream cheese bar should be divided into 16 equal pieces. Each should be rolled into a ball with clean hands.
2. Place the gelatin on a plate, and then coat each ball with the powder by rolling it there.
3. Please keep them in the refrigerator in an airtight container.

Nutritional Info: 174 cal, 16g fat (6g sag. fat), 31mg chol, 244mg sod, 4g carb (2g sugars, 0.9g fiber), 3.9g pro.

Coconut Sweets

(Preparation Time: 5 minutes | Cooking Time: 15 minutes | Serving 2 | Difficulty: Easy)

Ingredients:

- ¼ cup dry milk, non-fat

- ¼ cup unsweetened coconut, shredded
- 3 oz. ricotta cheese, non-fat
- ¼ cup plus 1 tbsp. sugar

Instructions:

1. Ricotta cheese should be heated in a sizable nonstick pan over medium heat. Stir well after adding the milk powder. Until most of the liquid has evaporated, cook for approximately 12 to 15 minutes. To prevent burning or to stick on the bottom, stir often.

2. Mix in the sugar. The Ricotta cheese mixture should be reconstituted as the liquid.

3. Continue to cook for a further 5 minutes while stirring. Mix well after adding the coconut. Cook for another three to five minutes. The mixture has to be quite thick.

4. The mixture should be poured into the oiled pan and pressed with a spatula.

5. 1-inch diamond-shaped pieces are cut. As the mixture cools, it solidifies. After total cooling, remove from the pan.

Nutritional Info: 137 cal, 3g fat (2g sag. fat), 7mg chol, 52mg sod, 20g carb (16g sugars, 5g fiber), 6g pro.

Apple Sugarless Cookies

(Preparation Time: 5 minutes | Cooking Time: 15 minutes | Serving 2 | Difficulty: Easy)

Ingredients:

- ½ cup finely chopped apple, peeled
- ½ cup water
- 1 tsp. Cinnamon, ground
- ½ tsp. salt (optional)
- 1 tsp. liquid sweetener
- ¾ cup dates, chopped
- ½ cup raisins
- 1 cup plus 1 tbsp. flour, all–purpose
- 1 tsp. baking soda
- 2 eggs

Instructions:

1. Dates, raisins, apples, and water are combined in a big pot. Bring to a boil; then, turn down the heat, and simmer for three minutes. The heat is removed; let it cool.

2. Cinnamon, salt, baking soda, and flour should all be combined. Mix thoroughly after adding to the apple mixture. Add sugar and eggs to the batter.

3. Onto a baking sheet with nonstick coating, drop by teaspoons. Bake for ten to twelve minutes at 350°F.

Nutritional Info: 54 cal, 1g fat (0g sag. fat), 18mg chol, 24mg sod, 18g carb (4g sugars, 1g fiber), 1g pro.

Cinnamon Nuts

(Preparation Time: 5 minutes | Cooking Time: 6 minutes | Serving 2 | Difficulty: Easy)

Ingredients:

- 1 cup shelled pecans, and walnuts, both mixed preferred
- ½ teaspoon cinnamon, ground
- 2 tablespoons butter
- 2 tablespoons erythritol

Instructions:

1. Melt the butter in a large, heavy skillet on medium heat before adding the nuts. Cook for five to six minutes while occasionally stirring.

2. Then immediately remove the pan from the heat, add the cinnamon and erythritol, and mix to combine.

3. Although they are fairly good when chilled, you will like them most when they are warm.

Nutritional Info: 136 cal, 8g fat (1g sag. fat), 0mg chol, 0mg sod, 13g carb (12g sugars, 2g fiber), 3g pro.

Cheese-Lemon Mousse

(Preparation Time: 5 minutes | Cooking Time: 5 minutes | Serving 2 | Difficulty: Easy)

Ingredients:

- 1 tablespoon gelatin, unflavored

- 4 egg whites
- 8 ounces of cream cheese
- 1 egg
- 1 teaspoon lemon zest, grated
- 2 tablespoons cold water
- ¼ cup lemon juice
- ¼ teaspoon cream of tartar
- ¼ teaspoon liquid stevia
- ½ cup sour cream

Instructions:

1. In a small cup, first, add the water. Then, sprinkle the gelatin over the top to soften. Give it 10 minutes to sit.

2. Warm up your lemon juice by placing it into a small, nonstick saucepan over low heat. When the gelatin has softened, combine it with the lemon juice and mix until all of the gelatin's granules have been dissolved.

3. The egg whites must now be beaten. The egg whites won't whip if there is oil in the bowl, on the beaters, or even the slightest bit of yolk in the egg whites. When they are foamy, add the cream of tartar and continue beating until firm peaks form. As you complete the next step, set aside a minute or two.

4. Use an electric mixer to whip the stevia, cream cheese, and egg in a mixing bowl until the mixture is bubbly and light. The sour cream, gelatin mixture, and lemon zest are now added.

5. Gently incorporate the egg whites into the cream cheese mixture. The mousse should now be placed on lovely dessert plates and refrigerated for at least four to six hours before serving.

Nutritional Info: 596 cal, 61g fat (36g sag. fat), 185mg chol, 417mg sod, 6.2g carb (4g sugars, 0g fiber), 7g pro.

Berry Mixed Cups

(Preparation Time: 5 minutes | Cooking Time: 15 minutes | Serving 2 | Difficulty: Easy)

Ingredients:

- 1 cup boiling water
- ½ orange zest, grated
- 1 cup divided heavy cream
- 8 ½ g 1 package raspberry gelatin, sugar-free
- 2 teaspoons lemon juice
- ¾ cup frozen blackberries, thawed partly
- 12 drops liquid stevia

Instructions:

1. Blend the gelatin with lemon juice, water, and orange zest for ten to fifteen seconds to dissolve it. Just long enough to incorporate the blackberries add them and spin one more.

2. Just long enough for the mixture to thicken, place the blender container inside the refrigerator for about 10 minutes.

3. Run the blender for 10 to 15 seconds, just long enough to combine everything after adding 3/4 cup of heavy cream. Pour chilled mixture into 6 adorable dessert cups. Wash the leftover 1/4 cup of cream with liquid vanilla stevia for the garnish. Place a tablespoon on top of each dish.

Nutritional Info: 89 cal, 0g fat (0g sag. fat), 0mg chol, 0mg sod, 24g carb (20g sugars, 3g fiber), 1g pro.

Chocolate Strawberries Mousse

(Preparation Time: 2 minutes | Cooking Time: 5 minutes | Serving 2 | Difficulty: Easy)

Ingredients:

- 1 cup cold skim milk
- Whole strawberries, fresh
- ¼ oz. Instant pkg. chocolate fudge pudding mix, sugar-free
- 1 ¾ cup whipped light topping

Instructions:

1. Pudding mix plus milk should be well combined in a mixing dish; this should take 2 minutes.

2. Whip the topping in. Strawberries should be provided for dipping. Angel food cake pieces may also be placed on top.

Nutritional Info: 24 cal, 7g fat (4g sag. fat), 3mg chol, 70mg sod, 4g carb (3g sugars, 1g fiber), 1g pro.

Flan

(Preparation Time: 5 minutes | Cooking Time: 60 minutes | Serving 2 | Difficulty: Easy)

Ingredients:

- 1/3 cup erythritol
- ½ teaspoon liquid stevia
- 1 salt pinch
- 8 tablespoons caramel coffee flavoring syrup, sugar-free
- 2 cups heavy cream
- 1 teaspoon vanilla extract
- 6 eggs
- 1 pinch of nutmeg, ground

Instructions:

1. Set the oven to 350°F. A 10-inch pie pan should be greased.

2. When everything is well blended, add the cream, vanilla, erythritol, stevia, salt, eggs, and nutmeg to your blender.

3. On the rack of the oven, place a shallow baking pan. Then set the pie dish within it.

4. Fill the outer pan with water until it is approximately 1/2 inch from the pie plate's rim. The custard mixture should now be added to the pie dish.

5. Between fifty and sixty minutes, or till just set, in the oven.

6. The pie dish should be carefully taken out of the water bath and cooled for 30 minutes before chilling.

7. While you may flip the flan upon a dish and drizzle it with caramel syrup before serving, it's simpler to just cut it into wedges like a pie or scoop it out. To serve, still, drizzle some syrup over the top.

Nutritional Info: 452 cal, 13g fat (6g sag. fat), 265mg chol, 343mg sod, 73g carb (73g sugars, 0g fiber), 14g pro.

Banana Ice cream

(Preparation Time: 5 minutes | Cooking Time: 5 minutes | Serving 2 | Difficulty: Easy)

Ingredients:

- 2 bananas frozen
- 2 teaspoon cocoa
- 1 teaspoon cinnamon

Instructions:

1. Bananas may be frozen in pieces, processed in a blender after freezing, and served as ice cream with either half a teaspoon of cinnamon, one teaspoon of cocoa, or both.

2. Another option is to combine mashed banana with one tablespoon of almond butter; the resulting ice cream is just as wonderful.

Nutritional Info: 273 cal, 15g fat (9g sag. fat), 58mg chol, 106mg sod, 31g carb (28g sugars, 1g fiber), 4g pro.

Chocolate Chip Oatmeal Cookies

(Preparation Time: 5 minutes | Cooking Time: 10 minutes | Serving 2 | Difficulty: Easy)

Ingredients:

- ½ cup brown sugar, firmly packed
- 3 tsp. vanilla extract
- ½ tsp. baking soda
- ¾ cup rolled oats, quick cooking
- 1/3 cup softened margarine
- 1 egg
- ¾ cup flour, all-purpose
- ¼ tsp. salt
- 1/3 cup chocolate chips, semisweet

Instructions:

1. Set the oven to 375°F.

2. Brown sugar is added while beating at medium speed until the margarine is light and frothy. While beating thoroughly, add egg and vanilla.

3. Add salt, baking soda, and flour together. Mix thoroughly as you gradually add the flour mixture to the margarine mixture. Add chocolate chunks and oats by stirring.

4. Spray cooking oil on cookie sheets. Drop dough onto cookie sheets using 2 tablespoons, allowing approximately 2 inches between each cookie. Make around 3 dozen cookies out of the dough by dividing it accordingly. Bake for ten minutes or until golden. In an airtight container, store.

Nutritional Info: 101 cal, 4g fat (2g sag. fat), 3mg chol, 120mg sod, 14g carb (9g sugars, 1g fiber), 1g pro.

Brownies

(Preparation Time: 5 minutes | Cooking Time: 15 minutes | Serving 2 | Difficulty: Easy)

Ingredients:

- 1 cup butter
- ½ cup Splenda
- ½ cup whey vanilla protein powder
- 2 ounces baked chocolate, unsweetened
- ½ cup erythritol
- 2 eggs
- 1 pinch salt

Instructions:

1. Set the oven to 350°F. Apply nonstick cooking spray to an 8-inch square baking pan.

2. Melt the butter and chocolate together over the lowest heat setting in a double boiler or a saucepan over a heat diffuser. Stir well to incorporate. Scrape it into a basin for mixing.

3. Stir well after adding the erythritol before adding the Splenda. The eggs should then be added one at a time. Salt and protein powder should be combined.

4. Bake for fifteen to twenty minutes after pouring into the prepared pan. Avoid over-baking!

5. Allow cooling in the pan after cutting into 12 squares. Keep in the refrigerator in an airtight container.

Nutritional Info: 233 cal, 15g fat (3g sag. fat), 37mg chol, 172mg sod, 25g carb (24g sugars, 1g fiber), 3.1g pro.

Berries and Coconut whipped cream

(Preparation Time: 5 minutes | Cooking Time: 5 minutes | Serving 2 | Difficulty: Easy)

Ingredients:

- ½ lemons
- 1 teaspoon vanilla bean, ground
- Optional: 1 dash of nutmeg, cardamom, and clove
- 2 cups fresh berries
- 1 tin coconut milk, full-fat, overnight refrigerated
- 2 tablespoons lucuma powder

Instructions:

1. Put the coconut milk and cream in the refrigerator for the night to separate them. Keep it from shaking before opening.

2. Scrape the cream into the bowl after opening the coconut milk container. Use the milk you've preserved for smoothies and other dishes.

3. Add vanilla, lucuma powder, and cardamom. Use a hand mixer to whip the cream until it is frothy. Please put it in the refrigerator.

4. Berry cleanup and placement in serving glasses or bowls. Over the berries, squeeze the lemon. Top the berries with a generous serving of cream and serve.

Nutritional Info: 170 cal, 11g fat (9g sag. fat), 5mg chol, 210mg sod, 30g carb (16g sugars, 11g fiber), 2g pro.

Walnut Italian Cake

(Preparation Time: 5 minutes | Baking Time: 45 minutes | Serving 2 | Difficulty: Hard)

Ingredients:

- ½ cup divided erythritol
- 1 pinch cream of tartar
- Pinch of salt
- 12 ounces walnuts
- 4 eggs
- 2 teaspoons lemon zest
- 2 tablespoons erythritol, powdered for topping

Instructions:

1. Set the oven to 350°F. Apply nonstick cooking spray to a 9-inch springform pan, and then cover the bottom using a circle of parchment paper or a recyclable nonstick pan liner.

2. Put the S-blade on your food processor and add the walnuts. Pulse the nuts until they are finely minced. When the nuts have finely minced but not greasy, add Two tablespoons of erythritol and pulse once or twice.

3. Divvy up your eggs. Please do yourself a huge favor and separate each one into a tiny dish/cup before putting the white in the bowl you want to beat them in since even the least bit of egg yolk would cause the whites to steadfastly refuse to whip! In such a case, breaking a yolk solely affects the white. Hurry them in! In such a case, breaking a yolk solely affects the white.

4. Place the yolks in a wider mixing bowl and the whites inside a deep, narrow dish.

5. With an electric mixer, beat the egg whites to form firm peaks after adding a little pinch of cream of tartar. Place aside.

6. Beat egg yolks and the remaining 6 tablespoons of erythritol in a bigger dish for at least three to four minutes, ensuring the mixture is light yellow and extremely creamy. Salt and lemon zest should be beaten in.

7. To the yolk mixture, add the ground walnuts. Gently pour your batter into the prepared pan after including all the egg whites.

8. For 45 minutes, bake. When the cake is still hot, sprinkle on top with 2 teaspoons of powdered erythritol. After the cake has cooled, serve. To serve, cut into thin wedges.

Nutritional Info: 266 cal, 9g fat (1.6g sag. fat), 55mg chol, 369mg sod, 41g carb (27g sugars, 1g fiber), 5g pro.

Chocolate covered Fruits

(Preparation Time: 5 minutes | Cooking Time: 0 minutes | Serving 2 | Difficulty: Easy)

Ingredients:

- ½ cup Superfoods chocolate, melted
- 1 banana or 1 apple or 1 bowl of strawberries or whatever fruit for dipping
- 2 tbsp. Nuts (walnut, almond, Brazil nuts) or seeds (hemp, sesame, chia, flax meal), chopped

Instructions:

1. Cut a banana into quarters or an apple into wedges. Chop the nuts while the chocolate is melting.

2. Fruit should be dipped in chocolate, covered with nuts or seeds, and placed on a platter. Place the dish in the refrigerator to let the chocolate set before serving.

3. If you prefer fruit over chocolate, spread it with sunflower or almond butter, top it with hemp or chia seeds, and chop it into pieces before serving.

Nutritional Info: 52 cal, 2.7g fat (1.5g sag. fat), 0 mg chol, 1.2mg sod, 8g carb (6g sugars, 1g fiber), 1g pro.

Meal Plan 60 Days

Following is a meal plan that can be followed for two months.

Meal Plan	Breakfast	Snack	Lunch	Snack	Dinner
Day 1	Spinach, Greek Cheese, and Olive Omelet	Cheese Crackers	Glazed Salmon	Club Sandwich Salad	Turkey Super-Easy Divan
Day 2	Oatmeal Superfoods Breakfast	Eggs and Cauliflower Salad	Cioppino	Chicken Chips	Chipotle-Maple Glazed Pork Steaks
Day 3	Asparagus All'uovo	Wicked Wings	Feta, Lamb, and Spinach Burgers	Chicken Meat Pizza	Maple-Bourbon Glazed Pork Chops
Day 4	Monterey Scramble	Pecan Chicken Salad	Jakarta Steak	Cheese-Garlic Stuffed Mushrooms	Shrimp Scampi
Day 5	Yogurt Oatmeal Breakfast	Chicken Tacos	Pork Loin with Walnuts and Red Wine	Asparagus and Crab Soup	Cioppino
Day 6	Rodeo Eggs	Capers and Lemon Tuna Salad	Kalua Pig and Cabbage	Stracciatella	Chicken Burgers with Sun-Dried Tomatoes and Basil
Day 7	Tortilla	Crab-Stuffed Mushrooms	Weekend Thanksgiving Curry	Almond-Chicken Noodle Salad	Lamb Steaks with Olives, Lemon, and Capers
Day 8	California Omelet	Tuna Chinese-Style Soup	Roasted Tasty Chicken	Fish Eggs	Oven-Fried Chicken Chops
Day 9	Backward Pizza	Deviled Eggs	Balsamic Onions and Mustard-Grilled Pork	Pecan Chicken Salad	Grilled Salmon
Day 10	Cocoa Oatmeal	Broccoli Cheddar Salad	Citrus Vinaigrette Salmon	Cinnamon-Butter Crispi's	Tandoori Chicken
Day 11	Avocado and Monterey Jack Omelet	Spinach Strawberry Salad	Yucatán Chicken	Not Pea Soup	Beef Stroganoff

Day 12	Blueberry and Flax Vanilla Overnight Oats	Egg Salad	Chipotle-Maple Glazed Pork Steaks	Mushroom Cream Soup	Joe
Day 13	Goat Cheese and Smoked Salmon Scramble	Chicken Dilled Salad	Bacon-Chili Scallops	Tavern Soup	Herb-Lemon Chicken Breast
Day 14	Apple Oatmeal	Olive Soup	Kalua Pig and Cabbage	Crab-Stuffed Mushrooms	Chicken Diavolo Skewers
Day 15	Club Omelet	Cucumber, Quinoa, Cilantro Tabbouleh	Meatza	Fried Japanese Rice	Orange Coconut Oil Flounder
Day 16	Instant Quiche	Cauliflower Purée	Broiled Pan Steak	Tuna Salad	Herb-Lemon Chicken Breast
Day 17	Braunschweiger Omelet	Chicken Meat Pizza	Bacon-Chili Scallops	Quinoa Salad	Maple-Mustard Glazed Pork Steak
Day 18	Frittata	Quinoa, Asparagus, Red Peppers Salad	Beef Stroganoff	Almond Chicken Rice	Noodles and Creamy Chicken in a Bowl
Day 19	Rosemary-Parmesan Eggs	Caesar Shrimp Salad	Italian Chicken	Wicked Wings	Smothered Burgers
Day 20	Egg pizza crust	Cheese Nacho Crisps	Deviled Pollock	Sopa Tlalpeño	Spareribs Adobado
Day 21	Buffalo Wing Sauce Omelet	Mediterranean Salad	Creamy Horseradish Sauce Chicken	Stuffed Spinach Mushrooms	Italian Easy Beef
Day 22	Pomegranate Coconut Oatmeal	Chicken Broth	Balsamic Onions and Mustard-Grilled Pork	Mushrooms with Sun-Dried Tomatoes, Bacon, and Cheese	Shrimp Scampi
Day 23	Omelet with veggies	Stracciatella	Chicken Golden Triangle Kabobs	California Soup	Roman Lamb Steak
Day 24	Egg Muffins	Cheese Nacho Crisps	Festive Pork	Glazed Walnuts	One Pot Dinner

Day 25	Instant Quiche	Beef Broth	Baked Clams	Chicken Tacos	Grilled Salmon
Day 26	Egg pizza crust	Rosemary Walnuts	Yucatán Chicken	Cheesecake	Camembert Sauce Pork
Day 27	Salmon Smoked Scrambled Eggs	Tavern Soup	Jakarta Steak	Spanish Spicy Wings	Creamy Horseradish Sauce Chicken
Day 28	Steak and Eggs	Crab-Stuffed Mushrooms	Lime-Anaheim Marinade Sirloin	Tuna Chinese-Style Soup	Bacon-Chili Scallops
Day 29	Zucchini Pancakes	Cream Cheese Balls.	BANH MI Burgers	Wicked Wings	Orange Topped Chops
Day 30	Spinach, Greek Cheese, and Olive Omelet	Avocado Pomegranate Salad	Portobello and Sun-Dried Tomato Salmon Roast	Chicken Meat Pizza	Bleu Burger
Day 31	Egg Bake	Coconut Sweets	Camembert Sauce Pork	Cucumber Greek Salad	Meatza
Day 32	Oatmeal Superfoods Breakfast	Cream of Salmon Soup	Oven-Fried Chicken Chops	Crab-Stuffed Mushrooms	Kalua Pig and Cabbage
Day 33	Pancakes Naan Crepes	Chili Cheese Chicken Salad	Almond Chicken Rice	Bacon and Beef Rice With Pine Nuts	Jakarta Steak
Day 34	Egg Muffins	California Soup	Bacon-Chili Scallops	Sirloin Salad	Yucatán Chicken
Day 35	Buffalo Wing Sauce Omelet	Stuffed Spinach Mushrooms	Smothered Burgers	Spinach Strawberry Salad	Crab Cakes
Day 36	Pomegranate Coconut Oatmeal	Chicken Tacos	Glazed Salmon	Cheese-Lemon Mousse	Beef Pepperoncini
Day 37	Monterey Scramble	Berries and Coconut whipped cream	Italian Chicken	Cheese Nacho Crisps	Lime-Anaheim Marinade Sirloin
Day 38	Backward Pizza	Spanish Spicy Wings	Orange Topped Chops	Tortellini Soup	Dill Poached Trout

Day 39	Avocado and Monterey Jack Omelet	Asparagus and Crab Soup	Kalua Pig and Cabbage	Sour and Sweet Cabbage	Ginger Tokyo Pork Chops
Day 40	Cocoa Oatmeal	Lemon Chicken with Rice	Transcendent Flounder	Capers and Lemon Tuna Salad	Broiled Pan Steak
Day 41	Goat Cheese and Smoked Salmon Scramble	Cajun Pecans	Chicken Golden Triangle Kabobs	Chocolate Strawberries Mousse	Beef Stroganoff
Day 42	Yogurt Oatmeal Breakfast	Pesto Gorgonzola Caesar Salad	Herb-Lemon Chicken Breast	Cheese Crackers	Florentine Burger Scramble
Day 43	Braunschweiger Omelet	Spanish Spicy Wings	Zucchini Italiano Meat Loaf	Dragon's Teeth	Halibut with Herb-Lemon Sauce
Day 44	Blueberry and Flax Vanilla Overnight Oats	Asparagus Sesame Salad	Weekend Thanksgiving Curry	Chicken Tacos	Roman Stew
Day 45	Pancakes Naan Crepes	Flan	Italian Easy Beef	Cuke and Sour Cream Salad	Pesto Mayonnaise Salmon
Day 46	Tortilla	Gingered Monkfish	Jakarta Steak	Chocolate covered Fruits	Italian Chicken
Day 47	Rodeo Eggs	Wicked Wings	Bleu Burger	Cheesecake	Glazed Salmon
Day 48	Apple Oatmeal	Mushroom Risotto	Meatza	Cinnamon-Butter Crispi's	Bacon-Chili Scallops
Day 49	Rosemary-Parmesan Eggs	Berry Mixed Cups	Lamb Mediterranean Burgers	Sesame Sautéed Spinach	Garlic Cheese and Artichokes Stuffed Chicken Breasts
Day 50	Frittata	Crab-Stuffed Mushrooms	Dill Poached Trout	Cajun Pecans	Jakarta Steak
Day 51	California Omelet	Cinnamon-Butter Crispi's	Chicken Diavolo Skewers	Pineapple Curried Rice	One Pot Dinner
Day 52	Instant Quiche	Walnut Italian Cake	Beef Pepperoncini	Chicken Chips	Deviled Pollock
Day 53	Egg Bake	Rosemary Walnuts	Lime-Anaheim Marinade Sirloin	Tossed Favorite Salad	Camembert Sauce Pork

Day 54	Club Omelet	Moroccan Sizzling Shrimp	Creamy Horseradish Sauce Chicken	Chocolate Chip Oatmeal Cookies	Zucchini Italiano Meat Loaf
Day 55	Salmon Smoked Scrambled Eggs	Cheese Nacho Crisps	Balsamic Onions and Mustard-Grilled Pork	Pepperoni Chips	Pesto Shrimp
Day 56	Egg Muffins	Vegetable Broth	Wine Sauce Rib-Eye Steak	Cream of Salmon Soup	Chicken Diavolo Skewers
Day 57	Asparagus All'uovo	Cinnamon Nuts	Portobello and Sun-Dried Tomato Salmon Roast	Caesar Chicken Salad	Zucchini Italiano Meat Loaf
Day 58	Steak and Eggs	Banana Ice cream	Camembert Sauce Pork	Spanish Spicy Wings	Italian Chicken
Day 59	Zucchini Pancakes	Cheese-Garlic Stuffed Mushrooms	Italian Chicken	Brownies	One Pot Dinner
Day 60	Omelet with veggies	Apple Sugarless Cookies	Halibut with Herb-Lemon Sauce	Wicked Wings	Country Style Maple-Spice Ribs

Conclusion

A serious non-communicable illness with rising incidence worldwide is type-2 diabetes. Type-2 diabetes develops when the body cannot utilize the insulin it generates or produces insufficient amounts. The main factor contributing to early mortality is type-2 diabetes. If not treated appropriately, it may cause various health problems, such as heart disease, kidney illness, stroke, blindness, and nerve damage, amputations of the legs and feet, or even death. Although type-2 diabetes, often known as adult-onset diabetes, is the most prevalent and typically develops in a person's mid-50s, it is preventable.

Small lifestyle modifications may decrease your likelihood of contracting this condition significantly. Therefore, effort should be made to change the changeable lifestyle and dietary habits that impact the development of this illness to avoid it. However, increasing compliance with this pattern is of significant public health relevance since healthy eating, like a strategy encouraging walking, fitness, or other physical exercises, positively impacts human health and prevents diabetes. Whatever eating regimen or diet you decide to adopt, consuming a wide range of nutritious foods and exercising portion control is preferable. Limit your intake of foods rich in cholesterol, saturated fats, and added sugars.

This book includes 200 recipes to help you maintain a healthy diet. You may also get assistance from your physician or nutritionist in creating a sustainable meal-planning strategy that suits your requirements and way of life.

FREE BONUS: Diabetes Journal

As I promised you when you purchased the book, you can download a very useful diabetes journal for free.
With the journal you can monitor and keep track of all your diabetes related health parameters.
It is in digital format so you can print it out and store it neatly to keep track of everything you need. I am sure it will be very useful for you!

How to download the journal?

Is very simple!

1. **Send an email to <u>bonus.violetharmond@gmail.com</u>** and include *"Diabetes Journal"* as the subject line and *"I want my journal"* as the message text.
2. You will immediately receive an automatic email that will contain a link that will allow you to download your bonus.

Printed in Great Britain
by Amazon

24682933R00057